EVERYTHING
YOU NEED TO KNOW
ABOUT GRAMMAR

EVERYTHING YOU NEED TO KNOW ABOUT GRAMMAR

by Leo Hamalian & Frederick R. Karl

FAWCETT CREST • NEW YORK

EVERYTHING YOU NEED TO KNOW ABOUT GRAMMAR

Published by Fawcett Crest Books, a unit of CBS Publications, the Consumer Publishing Division of CBS Inc.

ISBN: 0-449-23680-3

Printed in the United States of America

10   9   8   7   6   5   4   3

Contents

INTRODUCTION—This brief handbook is an outgrowth of our work with Open Admissions students at the City College of New York. At first, we used the traditional handbooks of composition to teach grammar and correct writing. But it soon became clear to us that (1) our students could not learn from these handbooks; and (2) the handbooks were as much at fault as the students. Most rhetoric and grammar books that nearly every major publisher has on its list are weak as references and disastrous as texts. Only the student who already knows the grammatical issue at hand can understand the murky explanations that the authors advance. Definitions of verbals, modifiers, agreement of elements, verbs, conjunctions, and clauses, among others, are impenetrable. Often they are misleading.

For years we went along with these handbooks and imposed them upon generations of students; and as long as the students were from the top of their high-school classes, we never questioned the texts seriously. Any student who could not use the language precisely and correctly did not stay long anyway. But as the student body at City College, as elsewhere, began to include those who were less well prepared for college-level writing, we quickly saw how flawed our assigned texts were as teaching tools. These are not ignoble books; they strive very hard to inculcate good writing and correct usage. But as teaching devices, they are far off the mark, whether the student is from the top or the bottom of his class. Such texts are for another era.

Obviously, no single text can make a marked difference. Students need far more help than a book can furnish. Nevertheless, we felt that a readable handbook, arranged attractively for every reference, would be a partial solution to poor writing style and ignorance of grammatical principles. Although the entries are brief, there is no lowering of standards of usage. The English we stress is cultivated

English and standard, correct usage. Our aim has been to provide all necessary entries, clear definitions, and simple examples. Toward this end, we eliminated side issues, trimmed excessive explanations, and streamlined major points. By means of an alphabetical arrangement, we made all entries almost instantly accessible.

At the same time, we have tried to include more than the typical handbook offers. Many rhetorical or literary terms come up in basic writing courses—*protagonist, meter, rhythm, metaphor,* among others—and we have always sensed that the student needs a straightforward definition of such words. Our explanations are hardly the final word on such matters, but then beginning writing courses are hardly the final word either. We have tried to maintain a balance between no knowledge and profound knowledge. Most students learn grammar and literary terms on the run, while their free time goes into their compositions. We hope to catch them as they brush past.

Major topics include making an outline, writing a composition, planning and writing a research (library) paper, and writing a letter—all tasks that arise in the freshman year. For the instructor who wishes a more traditional course, the section at the end, called "A Course of Grammar," will demonstrate how the book can be used as a handbook. The exercises that follow are themselves tied to the examples in the text, so that an instructor seeking sentences for verbals or conjunctions or pronouns will have numerous opportunities for assignments. The index at the end will provide access to secondary points in the main categories.

Leo Hamalian

Frederick R. Karl

Grammatical and Rhetorial Terms

1.

A, AN—*A* is used before words beginning with consonants or pronounced with initial consonants, as: *a* day; *a* unique time. *An* is used before vowels, as: *an* ordinary day; *an* apple. Words beginning with a pronounced *h* may be preceded by either *a* or *an*, but *an* often sounds awkward, as *an* historical process.

Caution: Avoid the extra *a* or *an* when unnecessary, as: What sort of *a* person are you? (No *a.*)

Be sure to repeat *a* or *an,* as: I have *an* apple and *a* pear.

1.

ABBREVIATIONS—Avoid abbreviations except in manuals, footnotes, reference books, bibliographies, class notes, etc.

The most common abbreviations appear before names: Ms. Jones, Mrs. Smith, Mr. Green, Dr. Thomas. We never write: She is a dr. *Abbreviations can never designate a group or a class of people.* When used with the first name or initials of the persons, titles such as *Professor* and *Reverend* may be abbreviated: Prof. J. V. Hatch, the Rev. James Smith.

Abbreviations are usually followed by periods. Some exceptions are acronyms—UNESCO, etc.—or organizations—CBS, UFCT, FBI, etc.

If an abbreviation ends the sentence, use *only one* period.

1.

ABSOLUTE CONSTRUCTION—a construction (or phrase) that modifies (or goes with) a whole sentence or clause, as in:

1. *The game completed,* the players trooped off the field. (The absolute construction has its own subject and incomplete verb form, independent of the subject of the main clause.)

2. *His response given,* he left the room in a hurry.

1.

ABSOLUTES, COMPARISON OF—We sometimes call words like *equal, unique, infinite, perfect, round, circular, square,* etc. absolutes. Logically, they are final and cannot be qualified or compared. If a thing is unique, it is one of a kind. If it is complete, it cannot be further finished. Yet there are exceptions, as in the following comparison of perfect: In order to form a *more perfect* union . . . (*More nearly perfect* would be grammatically correct but would forfeit the harmony.)

On occasion, we use "more complete," or "fuller." On the other hand, the following should be avoided:

1. This table is *rounder* than yours. (Round is round.)
2. This is the *most unique* experience I've ever had. (You cannot go beyond *unique* itself.)

Matters of taste dictate usage here.

1.

ABSTRACTION—a general word or expression separated from a specific instance. Unskilled or unscrupulous writers will use abstract words as though they refer to concrete entities. We need certain abstract concepts (hence words) in order to communicate efficiently. Think of the headaches we would have if we could not refer to all the dwellings in a place by the word *houses* but, instead, had to name each individual house. Too often, however, we use abstract words like *democracy, justice,* or *liberty* as though they referred to specific entities. This fallacy could be defined as a failure to distinguish between abstract and concrete words. The objects referred to by *table* and *chair* can be pointed to; the ideas reprinted by *justice* and *truth* have no such specific reference. Abstract language, like metaphor, produces emotion. A statement such as "Justice triumphs over all" has emotional appeal, but it is too abstract to convey information *about any specific situation*. It might be "brought down the abstraction ladder" (to use a semanticist's words). Other examples of abstractions are:

1. That behavior violates human nature. (What is human nature?)
2. Science means progress. (What is progress? For whom? Under what conditions?)
3. Democracy safeguards our liberties. (Which democracy? Many dictatorships call themselves "people's democracies.")
4. Love conquers all. (In this statement, each word is abstract.)

1.

ADJECTIVE—a single-word modifier which usually appears before the *noun* it describes, as in: It was a *big* game. She is a *lovely* person. An adjective can also follow the linking verb, as in: The game was *big*. She seemed *lovely*.

Adjectives may also modify *pronouns,* as in: He is *tall*. They are *intelligent*.

Most adjectives can be compared by adding suffixes *-er* and *-est* to the adjective base. Almost all one-syllable and many two-syllable adjectives are compared this way:

>   big, bigger, biggest;
>   strong, stronger, strongest;
>   common, commoner, commonest.

Many two-syllable adjectives and all of three syllables or more are compared by adding the words *more* and *most:*

>   beautiful, more beautiful, most beautiful;
>   precious, more precious, most precious.

Certain adjectives are irregular:

>   good, better, best;
>   much, more, most.

Warning: Avoid the double comparative, such as: *more* neat*er, more* big*ger. Further warning:* Do not try to recognize an adjective from *form* alone: a *round* table ("round" is an adjective); in the third *round* (a noun); *round* the corner carefully (a verb).

1.

ADVERB—a single-word modifier usually describing a verb, as in: He hid it *carefully*. She walked *rapidly* and *apprehensively*. Adverbs may also modify or describe an adjective, as in: He was *very* tall. Or they may modify another adverb, as in: She worked *very* well.

The position of the adverb is often not fixed in the sentence; it can be freewheeling, modifying its key word from various positions in the sentence, as in these examples:

1. *Dutifully,* he performed the task. (*Dutifully* modifies *performed*.)

2. He *dutifully* performed the task. (Same function.)

3. He performed the task *dutifully*. (Same function.)

Since word order is not a clue in identifying adverbs, we try to recognize them *from their functions*. Adverbs function in sentences to answer three basic questions:

1. *Where?* In this group of adverbs, we have *somewhere, sideways, backward, there, outside, below, above*.

2. *How?* In this group, we have *quickly, slowly, brutally, fast, slow, smooth*. Note that the last three can also be used as *adjectives* (*which see*).

3. *When?* In this group, we have *yesterday, today, rarely, often, seldom, never*.

One common indication of substandard English is the substitution of adjectives for adverbs. The following sentences are all *incorrect:* He drove *reckless*. She talks *polite*. He writes *good*. He writes *more clearer*. (Correct forms: *recklessly, politely, well, more clearly*.)

Comparison: She works *more rapidly* than he. (Comparative form of adverb; note the *-ly*.) She works the *most rapidly* of all. (Superlative form; note the *-ly*.) He comes *nearer* than he should. (Comparative form; not

15

more near.) He comes the *nearest* of all. (Superlative form; not *most near.*)

Irregular forms: Mary does *worse* (not *less well*) than she should. Mary does the *worst* (not *least well*) of all.

1.

AFFECT, EFFECT—*Affect* is a verb meaning "influence"; *effect* is a noun meaning "result," as: He was not *affected* by the medicine. The *effect* was produced by the lighting.

Effect is sometimes a verb meaning "bring about," as: The victory *was effected* by a strong running game.

In psychological usage, *affect* is sometimes a noun meaning "state of emotion," or the feeling equivalent of an idea.

1.

AGREEMENT—A verb must agree with its subject in number and person; a pronoun must agree with its antecedent (or reference) in gender and number:

1. On the shelf there *were* six *books*. (Not *was,* since *books* is the subject of the sentence, not the expletive *there.*)

2. *Harmony* of color, no less than unity of details, *is required* for great painting. (Not *are required,* since *harmony* is the subject.)

3. He is one of those men who *hate* to cook. (Not *hates,* since the antecedent of *who* is *men,* which is plural.)

4. *Does either* of these arguments make sense? (Not *do,* since *either* is singular.)

5. *Alice* is a *person who* is true to *her* conscience. (*Her* agrees in gender and number with *Alice* and *person.*)

6. In the past, *man* has made extravagant sacrifices to satisfy *his* gods. (Not *their,* since the antecedent, *man,* is singular.)

7. *Everybody* must bring *his* (or *her*) books tomorrow. (*His* agrees with *everybody,* which is singular.)

1.

ALLUSION—a shorthand reference to characters and events of mythology, legends, history, or literature. Poetry in particular relies upon such associations. In one sense, education is the process of familiarizing oneself with allusions one is likely to encounter not only in books but in the world outside the classroom. *Herculean strength* alludes to the Greek strong man of antiquity, and when we say that a Rockefeller is *richer than Croesus,* we expect people to catch the classical allusion to the Lydian king of the sixth century B.C.

1.

AMBIGUITY—A statement that can be interpreted in more than one way is regarded as ambiguous. In poetry, ambiguity is often the poet's deliberate technique for enriching the meaning, but in *expository prose* (explanations of material) you should avoid ambiguity. Don't leave your reader to guess your meaning.

1.

AMONG, BETWEEN—*Among* is used when there are at least three distinct items, as: *among* the books, *among* all those people, *among* the boys. *Between* is usually reserved for two items, as: *between* the two courses. Examples:

1. The choice is *between* Republicans and Democrats. (Two items or groups.)
2. It is to be divided *between* you and me. (Two people.)
3. I scattered the money *among* the crowd. (More than two.)

1.

ANNOTATION—a commentary on a text (essay, poem, novel, etc.). Annotations include both a reader's notations in the margins of a page and an editor's printed criticism or commentary meant to clarify a passage. An *annotated bibliography* is a list of books, with each title followed by a comment on the contents.

1.

ANTITHESIS—a figure of speech in which ideas are so set out that they appear in sharp contrast to each other: "To err is human, to forgive divine." (Alexander Pope) "Better to reign in hell than serve in heaven." (John Milton)

1.

ANTONYM—a word that means the opposite of another word. *Short*, for example, is the antonym of *long*, *present* of *absent*, etc.

1.

APOSTROPHE—a mark of punctuation that has three basic uses: (1) to indicate the possessive case of nouns; (2) to indicate the omission of a letter or letters in contractions; (3) to indicate a dropped letter in dialogue.

1. The *possessive* is formed in the singular by adding *'s* to the base word: the *man's* hat, the *lady's* coat, the *student's* pass. The possessive plural is formed by adding the apostrophe after the final *s:* the *students'* pass, the *ladies'* coats. But: the *men's* hats—because the plural of *man* is *men,* without a final *s.* To show possession for a name ending in *s,* add *'s,* as in Keats's poetry. If the result is difficult to pronounce, avoid the final *s,* as in: *Moses'* Tablets, not *Moses's.*

2. *In contracted words,* the apostrophe is used to show that one (or even more than one) letter has been omitted: *there's,* for *there is; there're,* for *there are; can't,* for *cannot.* Do not confuse the contraction *it's* (it is) with the possessive pronoun *its* (The dog licked *its* tail); do not confuse the contraction *there's* with the possessive pronoun *theirs,* or *they're* with *their* and *there.*

3. *In dialogue,* the apostrophe indicates a dropped letter: "Better get *'long,*" he said.

Also, an apostrophe is a figure of speech in which a person not present or even an abstraction is addressed: "Milton! thou shouldst be living at this hour." (Wordsworth).

1.

ARGUMENTATION—a genre of the essay (or theme) in which the writer tries to make the reader agree with his point of view on some issue. Characteristics of argumentation: presenting reasons for one's position, drawing conclusions from the facts, applying the results to the case under discussion in a coherent and persuasive style. A newspaper editorial is a disguised form of argumentation, as are political speeches and most magazine articles. Finally, advertising is itself a form of argumentation, although often corrupt and calculating. The aim of argumentation, whatever the particular form, is to *persuade* the reader or listener.

1.

ARTICLE—As an adjective, the article is to indicate the presence of a following noun. Articles are defined as definite (*the*) and indefinite (*a, an*). All articles are adjectives. *A* appears before consonant sounds; *an* before vowel sounds. When an initial *h* or *u* is pronounced, introduce it with *a*, not *an: a* historical event, *u* unique gift.

1. Use *a* when you mean any one of a whole class, as in: I have *a* pen and *a* book.

2. If *a* would be used without another adjective, keep *a* when using other adjectives, as in: It is *a* small red book. (Not: It is small red book.)

3. Use *a* in expressions of time or measure: *a* number of men; *a* little longer; *a* few hours.

4. Use *the* when you form the superlative degree of an adjective: *the* most beautiful picture, *the* longest day.

5. When pointing out something well known to both the writer and the reader, use *the: the* news, *the* office, *the* sky.

6. When using geographical names and other proper adjectives, use *the: the* Mexican border, *the* French Riviera, *the* Big Apple.

7. When pointing out a particular thing, distinct from all others of the same kind, use *the:* Give me *the* pencil on *the* table.

8. *No article* is necessary with nouns that cannot be counted so called mass nouns, such as *tea, money, sand, electricity* (all concrete things), or *life, work, courage, peace* (all abstractions).

9. When speaking of a customary action, no article is used: I go to school Tuesdays and Thursdays. After school, I go home.

10. If you would use *a* in the singular, use no article in the plural: *A* peach is on the table. Peaches are on the table.

1.

ATMOSPHERE—The atmosphere of a story is produced by several factors: descriptive detail, the tempo (rapidity or slowness) of the action, the degree of clarity of the events, the quality of the dialogue, *and, most important, the language the author chooses to use*. In brief, atmosphere may be defined as the dominant emotion which pervades the story. Presumably, every story has some degree of atmosphere. In many it is barely perceptible; in others, such as Shirley Jackson's famous story "The Lottery," it is the most striking feature of the plot. The skillful author uses atmosphere in support of other aspects of his narrative to create a unified effect. For instance, in O. Henry's "The Gift of the Magi," the atmosphere is deliberately cheerful in order to create contrast with the climactic events and so produce the wry kind of irony O. Henry delighted in. Atmosphere is related to *tone* (*which see*) but distinct from it.

1.

AWKWARD—a term to describe writing that is unidiomatic or otherwise stylistically flawed. Though no specific rule of grammar or syntax may be violated, the writing may be obscure, clumsy, ambiguous, wordy, or careless in sentence structure. Rewriting the statement in more direct and straightforward language may help to avoid the following examples of awkwardness.

1. *Clumsy order of elements:* On first sight, he seemed to be twitching, slightly built, and grinning in a foolish way. (Cut out *slightly built* and put it in a different sequence.) He wants three things: wealthiness, the love of women who are beautiful, and power. (Set up a clearer series: He wants wealth, power, and the love of beautiful women.)

2. *Insufficient or excessive subordination,* especially when it involves awkward repetition of a connecting element: Ulysses was very wily and lived on the island of Calypso for a long time and persuaded her to release him and then headed for home. (Better: After living on the island of Calypso for a long time, the wily Ulysses persuaded her to release him and then headed for home.)

3. *Using an element that may be understood or replaced by* another part of speech: Helene would play the violin, but whenever she played the violin, the dog would start to sing. (Better: . . . but whenever she did, the dog . . .) Iago is a puzzling character, but the force of Iago's hatred is ultimately inexplicable. (Better: . . . but the force of his hatred is . . .)

4. *Excessive duplication,* of words, or of sounds, or of words with the same prefix or suffix: Although his own *personality* is bland, he reveals the *personality* of others. (Try *temperament* in place of *personality*.) Other examples: As a minor *character* in the film, he helps to develop the *character* of the other *characters*. At any *rate,*

29

we all agreed that the *toll rate* was too high. The Jets *might* unleash their *might* any week. The Secretary of *State's statement* caused *static*. Has it *actually* been *officially* announced?

2.

BECAUSE—means *the reason is that.* Avoid *the reason is because;* use *The reason is that.* Sometimes *because* is shortened to *'cause,* but this form is inappropriate to writing. *See also* SINCE.

2.

BEGGING THE QUESTION—a form of circular reasoning that consists of repetition in the premises and the conclusion. For instance, it is obvious in the following argument: "Dickens is a good writer." "Why?" "Because he is very good—that's why." Here the conclusion does no more than repeat the premise.

Begging the question is usually not this crude. Often the premise is repeated but in different words: "Dickens is good." "Why?" "Because he is effective." The words *good* and *effective* are really the same here, and therefore the argument is still circular.

2.

BIBLIOGRAPHY—*See* RESEARCH PAPER.

2.

BRACKETS ([ ])—Brackets are used for two purposes: (1) to mark an error in the original through the use of *sic;* (2) to insert comments within a quotation from another writer.

1. *"The Dry Savages* [sic], the third of Eliot's *Quartets,* tells about a journey."* (Since the correct title is *The Dry Salvages,* the *sic* indicates that the spelling error appears in the original quotation and is being reproduced faithfully.)

2. The Secretary of State said, "Angola [which is twice the size of Texas] is necessary for American security." (The writer has added his own comment to the quotation. He must do so in brackets, because if he used parentheses instead, the comment would be taken as part of the original.)

3.

CAPITALS—Capital letters are most commonly used to begin a sentence, in proper names (Einstein); in titles of books (*The Invisible Man*), plays, films, articles, and poems; in titles of persons occupying high office (Prime Minister). When you title your composition or paper, you should capitalize *every important word: My Analysis of a Weekly News Item, The Meaning of Yeats's "Leda," Life with My Family.*

3.

CASE—the form of a *noun* or *pronoun*—usually *its ending*—which indicates its grammatical relation to other words. With nouns, there are few problems: we have the common or basic form and the possessive case: *man* as the common form, which becomes in the possessive: *man's* and *men's*. (If you are uncertain about the possessive of nouns, *see* APOSTROPHE.)

With pronouns, the use of case becomes trickier. After a *linking verb* (*to be, is, are, was, were*), formal English calls for the subjective or nominative case: It is *I*. (Not *me*.) Had it been *they* I would have come sooner. (Not *them*.)

The object of a preposition and the object of a verb are always in the objective or accusative case: Between you and *me*, John is wrong. (Not *I*.) The book is dedicated to George and *her*. (Not *she*.) I saw *him*, and at the same time she observed *them*. (Not *he*, not *they*.)

Another problem involves *who* and *whom*. *Who* is used in all subject situations; *whom* is used in all object situations. As: *Who* is on the phone? (*Who* as subject of the verb.) *Whom* do you want to speak to? (*Whom* as object of the preposition.) The actor *who* I think is best is ill. (*Who* as subject of *is best*.) With *whom* are you going? (*Whom* as object of *with*.)

3.

CHARACTER—Since fiction (*which see*) deals with changing human relations, the representation of persons is perhaps the most important element. Even when characters are animals, they represent human beings or exhibit human attributes.

We can distinguish between *static* and *developing* characters. The static character, a holdover from the Elizabethan "humors," remains essentially unchanged throughout the action. Because he is not directly involved in the changing human relationships, he plays a supporting role in the action. At the heart of the narrative, there is usually a *developing* character, who changes in personality or grows into new awareness of life. For instance, Gudrun and Ursula in Lawrence's *Women in Love* develop, in contrast to Hermione.

The method of characterization is either *expository* or *dramatic*. The expository method tells about the character. He is described or discussed by the author or another character. The dramatic method shows us the character in action. From his behavior, his speech, and his recorded thought, we make deductions about his personality, his attitudes, and his relations with the other characters.

Another aspect of character is the function performed. The principal figure who commands our emotional allegiance is called the *protagonist*. The popular terms *hero* and *heroine* describe one kind of protagonist—the admirable person who embodies our ideals and who enjoys our sympathy or empathy. Since story is generated out of conflict, the representative of the opposing force in the struggle is called the *antagonist* (the popular term is *villain*, to designate a character whom we despise).

Often the writer finds it convenient to contrast the behavior of the character with another, called a *foil*, or to reveal his innermost thoughts through a *confidant* (*confidante*—female). Both are secondary characters.

3.

CLAUSE—A clause, by definition, must contain *a subject and a verb*. If it has both, it is a clause no matter what else you may notice about it. There are two types of clauses: *main* clauses (also called *independent*) and *subordinate* clauses (also called *dependent*).

Main clauses may stand by themselves and are punctuated with a period or with a semicolon (if the sentence is to continue). Example: He saw the results of his work. (The subject is *he*, and the verb is *saw*; the rest of the sentence is part of the main clause.) Example: *He saw* that he was too old for the job. (The subject is *he*, and the verb is *saw*; the rest of the sentence is a subordinate clause, not part of the main clause.)

Subordinate clauses may *not* stand by themselves—they must always be attached to a main clause or they will be fragments. Many familiar words introduce subordinate clauses; for example: *that, what, who, until, because, as, if, since, when*. Here are some examples:

1. He saw *that he was too old for the job*. (That introduces the subordinate clause; its subject is *he* and its verb *was;* the entire subordinate clause acts as a direct object of the main verb, *saw*.) *The clause serves as a noun* (a noun clause).

2. *When she came home from work,* she felt too exhausted to undress. (*When* introduces the subordinate clause; its subject is *she* and its verb *came*; the entire subordinate clause acts as a modifier of the main verb, *felt*.) *The clause serves as an adverb* (an adverbial clause).

3. I immediately saw a person *who filled my heart with hope*. (Who introduces the subordinate clause; it serves as subject of the clause, and its verb is *filled;* the entire subordinate clause acts as a modifier of *person* in the main clause.) *The clause serves as an adjective* (an adjective or adjectival clause).

Subordinate clauses, then, are of three types, but all three share common features—a subordinate word, a subject and verb, and a dependency on something in the main clause.

3.

CLICHE—a worn or trite expression, a stereotype (from a stereotype plate used in printing, thus something repeated, not fresh). Before a phrase becomes a cliché, it may be fresh and meaningful; then after repeated usage, it loses its appeal and becomes a cliché. Some clichés: *nipped in the bud, dead as a doornail, point with pride, the weaker sex, my better half, the groves of academe, drunk as a lord.* It is better to use the straight descriptive word than to substitute a cliché. The repeated use of clichés drags down the writer's meaning; he becomes tedious and repetitive. Another way of dealing with a cliché is to manipulate it into something original, as Oscar Wilde did in "Nothing succeeds like excess" ("Nothing succeeds like success") or "the author changes horses in mid-theme." This practice should not be overdone either.

3.

COLLOQUIAL—The word refers to the spoken language rather than the written language, and it means a kind of informal expression. Informal English derives its vocabulary and syntax from colloquial language and presents problems when it is used in a formal context. Some colloquialisms used in everyday speech are *get, got, fix* for *mend,* even *ain't* for *am not.* Formal English should be used in a letter of application, a report to colleagues or teachers, a invitation, a term paper, a thesis or dissertation, and in most school situations where the written word is required.

3.

COLON—a useful mark of punctuation that is often ignored by unpracticed writers. It may be used:

1. after the salutation in formal letters, as: *Dear Sir:* or *Gentlemen:*

2. to introduce a quotation in a sentence when that quotation is not closely linked to the sentence, as: At this time, he allegedly reported: "I can resist anything but temptation."

3. to introduce a quotation of more than five lines, especially in term papers or reports.

4. to restate, explain, or illustrate a statement, as: I like three qualities in his work: its wit, its brevity, and its clarity.

5. to set off a series of words, phrases, or clauses from the previous part of the sentence, as: Buy the following items: oats, barley, and rye.

3.

COMEDY—The term can be used for any work of the imagination from a play to a poem and including the film and the novel. Comedy is a form that is less exalted and less terrifying than tragedy. It commonly deals with ordinary people in farcical or laughter-provoking situations; it may also deal with upper or lower classes and be a so-called *comedy of manners*. Comedy almost always has a happy ending; and its chief aim is to amuse or entertain. The term is broad enough to cover the ribald, satirical drama of Aristophanes, the spiritual quest of Dante, the intrigues and ineptitudes of Congreve's characters, and the barbed wit of George Bernard Shaw. Comedy may be serious, but it is rarely solemn or morbid.

3.

COMMA—Because the comma seems so negligible, it has become the most misused mark of punctuation. It is not used for every pause; it is not used for breath control; and it is not used arbitrarily. Its functions are attached to specific instances. Keep in mind that the comma acts as *part of the meaning* of a statement; it is *not* extra or ornamental. It is, also, a mark of courtesy. Through correct comma use, you tell the reader what to expect. The major uses, with examples, follow:

1. The comma separates coordinating (equal) main clauses: John had to go to work, *but* Mary was able to head for school. (Comma before the coordinating conjunction connecting main clauses.)

2. The comma follows a fairly long introductory clause: *When she had finished with her chores,* she was able to rest for the first time during the day.

3. The comma follows an introductory phrase to avoid confusion: *As a result of her work,* she felt confident. Or: *To get down to basics,* he decided to start at the beginning. Or: *Having completed the research,* she left the laboratory.

4. The comma separates items in a series: Helen wanted to buy *skis, boots,* and *poles.* Or: They had several things to do: *buy baby clothes, shop for food,* and *get hold of some firewood.* The comma before the *and* can be omitted: Helen wanted to buy *skis, boots and poles.* If you omit this comma (called the *final serial comma*) in your writing, you should do it consistently, except in a complicated series where the comma helps present misreading.

5. The comma indicates apposition: Mr. Smith, *our milkman,* came late on Tuesday.

6. The comma sets off an interrupter: It was unfortunate, *on the other hand,* that we had no chance to go that day.

7. The comma is used in conventional places, such as in

44

dates. (April 10, 1927), in letter salutations (Dear Gloria,) and closings (Sincerely yours,), before a direct quotation (He said, "Why?"), in numbers (1,356), in addresses (Albany, New York), to separate names from titles and degrees (Sylvia Smith, Ph.D.; Joseph Healy, Jr.; Mary Johnson, D.D.S.), etc.

One area in which the student must decide whether or not to use a comma or commas arises with *restrictive* and *nonrestrictive* materials. *Restrictive* material (a word, phrase, or clause) is necessary for the overall sense; without this material, there would be a significant change of meaning in the larger unit. *Nonrestrictive* material, on the other hand, can be dropped out without any real change of meaning. Such *nonrestrictive* material would appear in commas if within the sentence or with one comma if at the end or at the beginning. Examples:

1. The novel *which I liked the best* was *The Scarlet Letter.* (Your decision about commas would come with *which I liked the best*—there are no commas around it because this *restrictive clause* is necessary for the meaning.)

2. *The Scarlet Letter, which is my favorite novel,* was written by Hawthorne. (*Which is my favorite novel* does not affect the main meaning, which is that this novel is by Hawthorne—thus, the commas are used around this *nonrestrictive* clause.)

3. I should really like to come to your party, *although I may not be able to.* (The trailing subordinate clause is unnecessary to the main meaning, and the comma indicates that it is a nonrestrictive element.)

4. I wish, *however,* to arrive on time for this event. (*However* is here an interrupter or a transitional word, but unnecessary or nonrestrictive—thus, the commas are used around it.)

Before you leave this entry, try to justify every use of the comma in the explanations.

3.

COMMA SPLICE, COMMA FAULT—A comma splice or fault occurs when two independent word groups (main clauses) are joined by a comma only, as in: It is cold outside, I am going for a walk anyway. To correct a comma splice:

1. Add a connecting word: It is cold outside, *but* I am going for a walk anyway.

2. Replace the comma with a semicolon: . . . outside; I am going . . .

3. Replace the comma with a semicolon and a connecting word: . . . outside; *nevertheless,* I am going . . .

4. Replace one of the main clauses with a subordinate clause: *Although it is cold outside,* I am going for a walk anyway.

5. Replace the comma with a period, making two separate sentences: It is cold outside. I am going for a walk anyway. (This solution is the weakest, for you create two baby sentences with little connection between them.)

3.

COMPOSITION—writing a paper of 300–400 words. The topic here will be: Student Rights in a College-Level Course.

Settle your approach to a topic that is given in class or to your own topic if none is given. You may start out by being vague and unsure.

1. *Well before you start writing,* make a list of possible points you may use, *in any order* you wish. (Some of these may be discarded later.) For example:

A. kind of course (English, math, history, or any course; courses in general)

B. ground rules—lecture, discussion, reading of student papers

C. attitude and tone of teacher (traditional, open or closed manner, etc.)

D. basic or required course, elective, seminar

E. how you feel about the material

F. kind of material—long reading list, excerpted material, newspapers, magazines

G. requirements—several papers, journal, class report, midterm, final examination

H. your expectations of the course

I. the teacher's outline of the material and his expectations

J. type of college—vocational programs, academic, high or low pressure, junior, senior, community

2. *You need paragraphs,* and you should figure on at least 75 words for a paragraph. Some may be shorter, some longer, but 75–100 words is a good average. Aim for that. For 300–400 words, you will need three or four paragraphs. More than four will require a longer paper, and fewer than three will not permit adequate development. *Group the items on your list to provide paragraphs.* For instance, H & I seem to fit naturally; then A & B; possibly

C & G, adding J.; finally, E & F. Another arrangement is very possible, but make sure you have *enough material to support good-sized paragraphs.*

3. *You need a topic sentence* to start your composition and to provide a theme for the entire development of the paper. It should be a solid, inclusive sentence, such as: "The student has as many rights in a college course as does the instructor, and they should face each other as equals." That will be your theme all through. There is no changing it later. Then you begin the development of that sentence immediately, with points H & I (or any other suitable grouping):

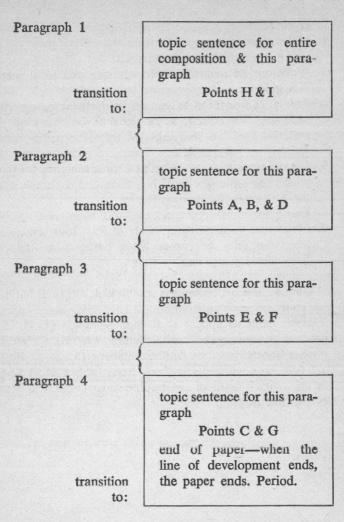

Paragraph 1

> topic sentence for entire composition & this paragraph
>> Points H & I

transition
to:

Paragraph 2

> topic sentence for this paragraph
>> Points A, B, & D

transition
to:

Paragraph 3

> topic sentence for this paragraph
>> Points E & F

transition
to:

Paragraph 4

> topic sentence for this paragraph
>> Points C & G
>
> end of paper—when the line of development ends, the paper ends. Period.

transition
to:

No summary or concluding paragraph.

Reminders:

1. Make a list of items.
2. Group them for your paragraphs.
3. Work out an inclusive topic sentence and let it serve as a guide.
4. Provide a transition as you go to the next paragraph, such as: "Of course, a lot depends on the kind of material you are studying"—a transition from paragraph 1 to paragraph 2.
5. Let the transition also serve as a topic sentence for that paragraph—the *of course* is a transitional phrase, and the rest gives the topic sentence.
6. End when your argument ends—no summaries.
7. Make sure your paragraphs are at least four sentences long. No one- or two-sentence paragraphs—that is baby thinking and baby writing.

Outline: If a list of items is insufficient, a formal outline for your composition follows:

Main elements appear as Roman numerals (I, II, III, etc.); subelements as capital letters (A, B, C, etc.); further subelements as Arabic numbers (1, 2, 3, etc.); still further subelements as small letters (a, b, c, etc.) *Keep in mind:* each level of the outline must contain at least two elements.

TITLE

I. Main element
 A. Subelement ⎫
 B. Subelement ⎭ at least two
  1. Further subelement ⎫
  2. Further subelement ⎭ at least two
   a. Still further subelement ⎫ at least
   b. Still further subelement ⎭ two

II. Main element
 A.
 B.
 C.
  1.
  2.

III. Main element
 A.
  1.
  2.
 B.

3.

COMPOUND SUBJECT—the collective term for two or more nouns or pronouns (or words used as nouns) that are the subject of the same verb. Examples:

1. *Jack* and *Jill* went up the hill. (Nouns as subjects.)
2. *He* and *I* helped to win the war. (Pronouns as subjects.)
3. *To dream, to strive,* and not *to yield* is important for our people. (Infinitives as subjects.)
4. *What the best have thought* and *what the best have written* is the material of literature. (Noun clauses as subjects.)

3.

COMPOUND VERB, COMPOUND PREDICATE—The collective term for two or more verbs joined by a coordinating *conjunction* (*which see*) and having the same subject. Examples: Tom *washed* and *ironed* his clothes. I *pushed, pulled,* and *tugged* to no avail.

3.

CONJUGATION—change in the form of a verb (*only a verb*) to indicate *tense, voice, mood, number,* and *person* (*see all*). Examples:
1. He *saw* the bird. (tense—past)
2. The bird *was seen* by him. (voice—passive)
3. *See* the bird. (mood—imperative)
4. He *sees* the bird. (number—singular)
5. They *see* the bird. (person—third)

3.

CONJUNCTION—a word that connects words, phrases, or clauses (sometimes called a connector or connecting word). There are three classes of connecting words. *Note the punctuation with each kind:*

1. *Coordinating conjunctions* (*and, or, but, nor, for, yet, so*) connect clauses of equal weight—that is, main clauses. As: John goes fishing, *but* Mary prefers tennis. I will leave early, *for* I cannot bear the sight of him.

2. *Subordinating conjunctions* (*although, when, if, unless, until, because, since, whenever,* and dozens more) join a dependent or subordinate clause to an independent or main clause. The clause with the subordinating conjunction becomes a subordinate clause. As: *When Mary comes home from college,* her family will celebrate with a big party.

3. *Conjunctive adverbs* are words normally used as adverbs which become connecting words: *however, nevertheless, consequently, thus, accordingly, moreover,* etc. As: George fell ill on the trip; *nevertheless,* he decided to continue to the next stage. I came early; *however,* I cannot stay long. (Note the semicolon when the conjunctive adverb is used in that position as a connector.) *Warning:* Such an adverb is not always conjunctive: Because it was late, *however,* she could not remain at the party. (In this sentence, *however* is not a connector, but simply a modifier or a transitional word.)

3.

CONNOTATION—the implications or suggestions in a word (as opposed to the strict dictionary meaning of the word—*see* DENOTATION). Connotations may be personal or objective; they may have pleasant or unpleasant associations; or they may be culturally conditioned, as in the word *communist,* which can refer to a radical, an economic theory, a country such as the Soviet Union, or an American traitor, as McCarthyism labeled Communists and suspected Communists in the 1950s. A recent word rich in connotations is *hippie,* although in future years the word may lose most of its implications.

3.

CONTACT CLAUSE—a clause in which the connective has been omitted. *I know* [*that* omitted] *he will show up* is correct usage, because *that* is unnecessary. However, *I recognize* [*that* omitted] *your right to raise such a question is legitimate* requires the *that* to avoid confusion of meaning.

3.

CONTRACTION—a fused word from which a syllable has been omitted, as: *won't* (will not), *can't* (cannot), *didn't* (did not), *isn't* (is not). The place of the omitted letter or letters is indicated by an apostrophe. As a rule, contractions are not used in formal English, but they are appropriate in informal English. Certain contractions (*they're, you're*) are often confused with other words (*their* or *there, your*) and should be used carefully.

4.

DANGLING MODIFIER—When the word to be modified is altogether absent or out of position, the modifier is called *dangling*. Sentence elements such as participial phrases, prepositional phrases, infinitive phrases, appositives, and entire clauses are liable to misplacement. The following sentences illustrate some common errors in danglers:

1. *Hanging from a limb,* we saw a bird's nest. (Who or what was hanging—we or the nest? Correct: We saw a *bird's nest hanging* from a limb.)

2. *Sorrowfully sobbing a denial,* John's chest heaved with emotion. (Can a chest sorrowfully sob? Correct: His chest heaving with emotion, *John sorrowfully sobbed* a denial.)

3. *To qualify for Little League baseball,* fathers must be cooperative. (Are the fathers to qualify, or their children? Correct: *If youngsters are to qualify* for Little League baseball, fathers must be cooperative.)

4.

DASH—This mark of punctuation (—) has three main functions:

1. to set off parenthetic or inserted statements which require extra emphasis, as in: Overusing the dash—as so many lazy writers do—is to deprive it of its ability to emphasize and clarify. (Commas would be less forceful.)

2. to signal a summary or appositive statement, as in: In brief, the novel succeeds—it entertains, instructs, stimulates. Or: He chose the last refuge of scoundrels—patriotism.

3. to indicate a shift or unexpected turn of thought, as in: They wanted power—not democratic government—and this they revealed after their victory.

DECLENSION—change in the form of a noun or pronoun to show *case, number,* and *gender* (*see all*).

Examples of case: *He* gave the *man's* hat to *him.* (*He,* nominative case; *man's,* possessive; *him,* objective or accusative.)

Examples of number: *He* and *they* have one *book* and two *pens.* (*He,* singular; *they,* plural; *book,* singular; *pens,* plural.)

Examples of gender: Give *it* to *him* or to *her.* (*It,* neuter; *him,* masculine; *her* feminine.)

4.

DENOTATION—the exact, particular meaning of a word, apart from emotional, political, or other associations. Words used denotatively should have no private or personal weight, but should be clear to all readers. *See also* CONNOTATION; AMBIGUITY; ABSTRACTION.

4.

DESCRIPTION—an account or a discourse in which the writer (or speaker) tries to capture a place, character, sensation, or an object. Description rarely appears alone. A theme or essay tends to move from one mode of expression to another: *describing* something prior to *explaining* its function; *narrating* an anecdote to support an *argument; presenting information* to the reader before beginning a story. A skilled writer of essays will draw upon all four basic modes: *exposition, narration, argument,* and *description* (*see all*).

4.

DIALECT—a variety of language usually transmitted orally and differing distinctly from the standard language. Dialect in English may be regional (general American, Scottish, Limey, New England, southern, midwestern, etc.) or cultural (educated, uneducated, ghetto, hillbilly, cultivated, etc.).

Some linguists maintain that standard English is merely the dialect of the educated and is no more expressive or logical than the dialect of ghetto blacks, of hillbillies, or of Outer Bank fishermen. They believe that calling one dialect "good English" is a political judgment, a way of reinforcing the bias that one element in society is destined to rule. That may be true, and every student has the choice to continue using dialect, but we should add that uneducated dialect is often imprecise in areas where precision is called for. A word like *hurtingest* may sound rich, but if we question its meaning, we are left at a loss. Some examples of dialect follow:

1. *Irregardless* of what he does, I am going. (*Regardless* is correct.)

2. If I had my *druthers,* I'd let it set for a while. (*Druthers* has no meaning in standard English, and *set* should be *sit.*)

3. He *begin* today. (Does the writer mean *began* or *begins?*)

In American English, dialectical differences mean matters of *grammar* (often incorrect in standard English), *vocabulary* (often enriching standard word patterns), and *pronunciation* (often carried over into incorrect spelling).

4.

DICTION—In writing, diction is the choice of words, especially with regard to clarity, correctness, and effectiveness. Although diction is a subject by itself for extended study, a few simple rules may be helpful:

1. Avoid trite expressions and other clichés: *fairer sex, acid test, psychological moment, by this I mean,* etc.

2. Avoid slang and overworked colloquialisms, except for special effect: *right on, hype, turn him on, doing your thing, having a ball, far out.*

3. Avoid vulgarisms and illiteracies: *anywheres, enthused, between you and I, irregardless, thusly, humans* (for *human being*), *amn't I.*

4. Avoid archaic and poetic language when unnecessary: *steed* (for *horse*), *must needs* (for *necessarily*), *amongst* for *among*).

5. Avoid genteel expressions and euphemisms: *repast, passed away, financial embarrassment, social disease* (for *venereal disease*), *alcoholic beverage.*

6. Avoid jargon unless there is no substitute: *communication skills, team teaching, task force, peer group, learning situation, the abovementioned.* Common sources of jargon are sports, business, advertising, and the social sciences.

4.

DICTIONARY—A dictionary will help you with *spelling, definitions, pronunciation, division of words into syllables, placement of accent or stress, acceptable usage, foreign words and phrases, etymology* (origin of a word), *synonyms,* and *antonyms.* Some warnings:

1. If you do not find the word you are seeking, do *not* use it anyway. You are misspelling it. Try another word that is similar until you can locate the correct spelling.

2. Make sure you choose the correct word, the one that fits your situation. Check the definition before you use an unfamiliar word.

3. The stress of a word is indicated by a small slant mark —do not confuse that with an apostrophe mark.

4. Do not confuse the division of a word into syllables with actual divisions when you write the word.

5. Make sure you break a word only between syllables; do not write *th-ought*.

6. Be certain your use of a word conforms to the part of speech given by the dictionary. If a word is only a verb, do not use it as a noun or an adjective.

4.

DIFFERENT FROM, DIFFERENT THAN—in formal usage, *different from* is considered correct, as in: He is different *from* me. In informal usage, however, *different than* has become common. *Differ* is always used with *from*, however, as: This *differs from* that.

4.

DIRECT DISCOURSE—a statement which reports actual words of someone speaking, as: She said, "I'll never give in to him." Direct discourse must always appear within quotation marks and should include all words and punctuation. *See also* INDIRECT DISCOURSE.

4.

DOUBLE NEGATIVE—a construction in which two words both convey the negative idea. Though such constructions were normal in Old and Middle English (Shakespeare used even triple negatives), they are frowned on today:
1. *No* one saw *nothing*. (Correct: No one saw anything.)
2. I *hardly* saw *nothing*. (Correct: I hardly saw anything. *Hardly* carries a negative sense.)
3. I did*n't* take *no* chances. (Correct: I didn't take any chances.)

5.

EITHER/OR—When used by itself, *either* is a pronoun in the singular, as in: *Either* is fine. When used as a connective with *or*, *either* may be singular or plural depending on the sense, as:

1. Either he or she is coming. (*She* determines singular *is*.)
2. Either they or he is guilty. (*He* determines singular *is*.)
3. Either Alice or the boys are the criminals. (*Boys* determines plural *are*.)

Keep consistent forms: *either/or; neither/nor*. Do not cross over.

5.

ELLIPSIS—This means some material is missing—words, phrases, or entire sentences. The ellipsis or missing material is indicated in print by three or four periods. If the missing or interrupted material comes in the middle of a sentence, use three periods: "John arrived whenever he wanted . . . but Alice came on time." If the material is omitted at the end or trails off, use four periods. The fourth period is the period for the sentence as a whole. "The truth of the matter is one cannot go back; some can, but. . . ."

5.

EMPHASIS—The two most emphatic positions in a sentence (and often in a paragraph or theme) are the beginning and the end. Since the subject and the verb are the most important elements, they should come close to the opening part of the sentence—unless, of course, the writer wants his emphasis at the end (a so-called *periodic sentence*). In the following sentences, emphasis can be improved:

1. However, the plot is implausible to most people. Try: The plot, however, to most people is implausible. Or: To most people, however, the plot is implausible. *Note:* The meaning often shifts a little when the emphasis changes.

2. In an instance such as this one, it would be preferable if I were offered the options of liberty or death. Try: Give me liberty or give me death. *Note:* The correct use of emphasis will eliminate unnecessary words.

Sometimes, you will deliberately repeat words to gain emphasis. An example of that occurs in Emile Zola's famous speech in defense of Dreyfus, in which each statement of the conclusion begins with "I accuse . . . "

In a paragraph, the *topic or key sentence* is most emphatic if it opens or concludes the particular paragraph. In a paper, the subject should be introduced in the opening paragraph and referred to in the concluding paragraph.

Keep in mind: Your emphasis, as much as content and tone, tells the reader how to read your work.

5.

EPIGRAM—a concise and pointed saying, made effective by its wit and ingenuity. It often uses *antithesis* (*which see*) or contrast. Coleridge's definition of this form is an epigram itself:

> What is an epigram? a dwarfish whole:
> Its body brevity, and wit its soul.

Oscar Wilde was noted for his epigrammatic statements: "I can resist everything but temptation." "An English fox-hunt—the unspeakable in pursuit of the uneatable." Epigrams often have no substance when paraphrased or explained.

5.

EPIGRAPH—a pertinent motto or group of words at the beginning of a book, chapter, or poem, often a clue to the meaning of a work. The epigraph from the *Satyricon* attached to T. S. Eliot's poem *The Waste Land* sounds the theme of spiritual imprisonment and the death wish. Do not confuse epigraph with *epitaph* (*which see*).

5.

EPITAPH—an inscription on a tomb or gravestone in memory of the one buried there, or a brief statement worded as if to be inscribed upon a monument. Amusing is the epitaph upon the passing of a young man named Longbottom: "Ars longa, vita brevis." Do not confuse *epitaph* with *epigraph* (*which see*).

5.

EVERYONE, EVERY ONE—*Everyone* means *everybody,* as in: *Everyone* is here. *Every one* means *each one,* as in: *Every one* of the apples is rotten. The same principle applies to *nobody, no body; everyday, every day; anyone, any one.* Examples: There is *nobody* here. There is *no body* to this wine. They come as an *everyday* occurrence. The mail arrives *every day.* Is *anyone* here? *Any one* of you will do.

5.

EXAMPLE—an instance serving to illustrate an abstract or general statement or idea. In clear and readable prose, *the writer alternates between abstract statements and specific examples.* As an obvious instance of example, we have the following statement: "The human spirit soars to infinity in the midst of darkness. For example, there are the compositions and statements of Beethoven, Kafka, and Helen Keller to inspire us." The first sentence is abstract and can lead anywhere; the second sentence illustrates with specific names examples of the human spirit soaring in the darkness. A third sentence would continue the concrete examples, and so on.

5.

EXPLETIVE—any word (but usually *there* or *it*) used so that it is grammatically independent of the construction in which it appears. It is used simply to get the sentence started.

1. *There* is a time to rejoice. (*There* is not the subject; *time* is the subject.)

2. *There* are times to rejoice. (*Times* is the subject and requires a plural verb, *are*.)

3. *It* is clear that he is sick. (*It* is not the subject; it simply gets the sentence started—*that he is sick* is the subject of the verb *is*.)

Do not confuse the expletive *it* with the pronoun *it*. The pronoun *it* will always have an antecedent or reference.

Do not confuse the expletive *there* with the adverb *there*. Example: *There* is a man over *there*. (The first *there* is an expletive; the second *there* is an adverb indicating where.)

5.

EXPOSITORY WRITING—The purpose of expository writing (also called *exposition*) is to inform the reader. It is directed primarily to the intellect rather than to the emotions, and this characteristic determines the formal level of diction, style, and the order of theme development. Though almost all writing in college (except for creative writing) is expository, often the techniques of narrative writing are employed to make the material more interesting. Some rhetoricians like to divide expository writing into such categories as analysis, description, criticism, and argument. *Primarily, though, exposition means the development of an idea so that information is presented to the reader.* There will be a minimum of description, no dialogue, and no creation of characters in this form. Expository writing may be narrative but it is not fiction (*see both*).

6.

FICTION—an imaginary but usually plausible prose narrative that dramatizes changes in human relationships, or in an individual character. It represents human beings or characters (*see* CHARACTER) in a sequence of events or psychological states. It normally has a beginning, middle, and end, but not necessarily in that order. Fiction will be presented in language, although the language of fiction may be factual, objective, poetic, romantic, etc.

Fiction takes many forms, among which are the novel, the novella (or short novel), the short story, and even the fable, fairy tale, and parable. A short story may be as brief as a three-line anecdote and a novel as long as a linked series of bulky narratives. Fiction may involve a single immobile character (as in Samuel Beckett's novels) or armies deployed over half of Russia (as in Tolstoy's *War and Peace*). It may be wholly dramatic or a mixture of action and essay. Although length is a factor, the scope and complexity of the work provide the basis of distinction among the forms. (A *roman à clef* is a type of fiction in which actual people and events are presented, although disguised.)

6.

FIRST PERSON SINGULAR—Personal pronouns change form according to their usage in sentences. The forms are called *case changes* (*see* CASE). When a personal pronoun refers to the *self*, it is the first person singular (*I, me, my, mine*) and will be in either the nominative case (*I*), the objective case (*me*), or the possessive case (*my* or *mine*).

Though these pronouns are among the most familiar in our vocabulary, people often fail to use them correctly in standard written English.

1. He likes science better than *I*. (This means: *better than I like science. I* is part of the subject.)
2. Jim and *I* decided to go. (*I* is part of the subject.)
3. Between you and *me*, I prefer not to go. (After the preposition *between*, use the objective case, *me*.)
4. Do you object to *my* going? (Avoid *me* here; the objection is to *going*, not to *me*.)

In writing, avoid overuse of *I, me,* etc. Use *a person, one, he, the writer;* try to put everything into the third person. Don't say "I enjoyed the play very much," but "Anyone seeing this play would enjoy it very much." Then plunge into concrete examples of why. (Another caution: In exposition or narration, avoid *you*—directed to the reader. Keep your material in the third person.)

6.

FRAGMENT—(A sentence fragment, also called a *period fault*), is the result of putting a period where one does not belong, and thereby writing as a separate sentence what is actually only a part of the sentence.

1. I got up early. *Looking tired and drawn.* (The italicized words cannot stand alone after a period; they go with the *I* of the preceding sentence.) Correct: I got up early, looking tired and drawn.

2. He decided to buy a small car. *Because the cost of gas had tripled.* (The italicized words cannot stand alone; they go with *decided* in the preceding sentence.) Correct: He decided to buy a small car because the cost of gas had tripled. Or: Because the cost of gas had tripled, he decided to buy a small car.

6.

FUSED SENTENCE—*See* RUN-ON SENTENCE.

7.

GERUND—The gerund *always functions as a noun,* although its form is the same as the present participle. By definition, *a gerund is a verb form used as a noun.* Examples of gerunds are:

1. *Playing* against the Vikings is difficult. (*Playing*—from the verb *play*—is used as the subject of the sentence.)
2. She hopes that *meditating* about life will cure her of worry. (*Meditating* serves as the subject of the subordinate clause.)
3. He likes *hunting* and *fishing*. (*Hunting* and *fishing* are used as direct objects.)
4. He is accused of *having left* the scene. (*Having left* is the object of the preposition *of.*)

Note that a gerund, unlike a participle, never modifies another word. A gerund is part of the class of words called *verbals*. Gerunds, participles, and infinitives are all *verbals,* which, although derived from verbs, never function as verbs. Note the distinction between verbal and verb:

1. She *was dancing* faster. (*Was dancing* is the verb whose subject is *she.*)
2. She began *dancing* faster. (*Dancing* is the verbal—gerund—which serves as the direct object of the verb *began.*)

7.

GRAMMAR—the study of how a language works. Its concerns are the function of words in a sentence (*see* PARTS OF SPEECH); the change of words to indicate function (*see* INFLECTION); and the relation of words to each other in a sentence (*see* SYNTAX). In English, there are three kinds of grammar:

1. *Historical:* the study of the development of language, how grammatical concepts and constructions evolve—for instance, the possessive apostrophe *'s* from the Old English genitive *es.*

2. *Descriptive:* demonstrates the way writers and speakers actually use language at the present time. Contemporary writing (newspapers, magazines, books) and contemporary speech (television, radio, speeches, conversation) are used in descriptive investigations.

3. *Prescriptive:* based on the "rules" that people *should use* in writing and speaking. (Some of this book is prescriptive.)

8.

HOWEVER—has two main uses: as a conjunctive adverb (that is, as a connector of two clauses) and as a parenthetical word.

As a *conjunctive adverb:* You can cut your classes; *however,* don't say I didn't warn you. (Note the semicolon before *however* in this usage.)

As a *parenthetical word:* Joyce, *however,* wrote most of his books about the land he left. (Note commas before and after *however.*)

8.

HYPHEN—A hyphen looks like this -. A dash looks like this —. Use a hyphen between the two parts of a modifier, as in: an *age-old* story, a *half-mile* run, a *three-foot* section, a *twenty-year-old* woman. (Note: the word *foot* and the word *year* remain singular—not *feet*, not *years*.)

A distinction: "This is a closely guarded secret." *Closely* is an adverb independent of *guarded*, not part of it; no hyphen.

Some nouns are hyphenated: X-ray, etc. Check your dictionary when in doubt. Many hyphenated words eventually become one word: *sales-man* became *salesman*.

9.

IDIOM—an expression that is peculiar to itself grammatically (as: *It's me*) or one whose meaning cannot be derived logically from its elements (as: *This car drives well* or *Monday week,* meaning *This car is easy to handle* and *Monday a week after Monday*).

Since rules for idiomatic expression are almost impossible to formulate, young writers are sometimes careless about curbing unidiomatic English. An unidiomatic expression is one that, without breaking any general rule of grammar or without producing any incongruity of meaning, is not proper English. Most commonly, it involves the misuse of a preposition or an article, as in:

1. In his paper, he uses *a great deal of* examples from history. (Correct: *a great many examples.*)

2. Before putting *the* pen to paper, you should think out your ideas. (Correct: *Before putting pen to paper.*)

3. He showed great strength to run. (Correct: *in running.*)

4. Between the two points of view, they preferred John's. (Correct: *Of the two points of view.*)

5. His job is one of a proofreader. (Correct: *He is a proofreader.*)

9.

IMAGE, IMAGERY—the term *imagery* (that is, "images" taken collectively) is used commonly in criticism, in two basic senses:

1. The term refers to descriptive passages in poetry, especially if the description is vivid and appealing to the senses. The passage does not have to be visual, but may appeal to hearing, touch, even smell. Shakespeare's Sonnet 30 begins with: "When to the sessions of sweet silent thought / I summon up remembrance of things past . . . " Or in Sonnet 116: "Love's not Time's fool, though rosy lips and cheeks / Within his bending sickle's compass come . . . "

2. It is also used to signify figurative language, especially similes and metaphors. For example, the entire following passage from Sonnet 29 may be considered an image: "Yet in these thoughts myself almost despising, / Haply I think on thee, and then my state, / Like to the lark at break of day arising / From sullen earth, sings hymns at heaven's gate; . . . " Some critics believes that images and "image clusters" contain the clues to the meaning, structure, and effect of a work. That is, the underlying theme or motif of a poem, a play, and even a novel must be found in its images.

9.

IMPLY, INFER—Although common usage has blurred the distinction, careful writers do distinguish between these words. *Imply:* Shakespeare *implies* that Othello is an egoistic idealist. Note that the subject of *implies* (Shakespeare) is the actor, the doer of the thing. *Infer:* However, not every reader *infers* the same thing. Note that the subject of *infers* (the reader) receives and carries out the action. One *implies* a point, but one *infers* from certain information.

9.

IN, INTO, IN TO—Though some grammarians insist that verbs of motion must be followed by *into*, it is safer to use your own sense of idiom or logic: Jump *into* bed! Jump *in* the lake!

In is distinct from *into:* We drove *into* New York. (But: We drove *in* for a play and dinner.)

The chief danger is that *into* will be used when *in to* is required: He may turn you *in to* the police. (Not *into.*) And sometimes *in* is used mistakenly when *into* is meant: He walked *into* the room unannounced. (Not *in.*)

9.

INDIRECT DISCOURSE—a statement that reports what someone said, but not in that person's words. As: She said that *she would never acquiesce to his demands*. (The *that* makes the statement indirect.) Indirect discourse is never enclosed in quotation marks. In a term paper, however, when a source is quoted indirectly, the paraphrase must be documented with a footnote. *See also* DIRECT DISCOURSE.

9.

INFINITIVE—a form of the verb, together with *to: to go, to be, to come, to see, to be seen, to have been seen.* Be careful not to use an infinitive as a verb; if you do, you will have a fragment, as: To go to the movies on Thursday with my friends, even if the weather is poor.

The infinitive acts as a noun in some sentences, as an adjective in others. As a noun: *To swim* is great pleasure. (The subject of the sentence is the infinitive.) As an adjective: The person *to see* is the instructor. (The infinitive here modifies person.)

The present infinitive indicates time simultaneous with or future to the time of the main verb, as: It is a joy *to read* his papers.

The perfect infinitive (*to have seen, to have come*) indicates time previous to the time of the main verb, as: He was sad *to have witnessed* such a sight.

Occasionally, the *to* part of the infinitive is omitted: They would rather (prefer to) *go* hungry than dare (dare to) *come* without the bags.

Some verbs take the infinitive form with or without *to,* as: We helped him (to) *win* the game. He can (is able to) *go.*

9.

INFLECTION—a general term for a change in form of a word to show number, case, gender, person, tense, voice, mood, or degree. In English, the inflection is either internal (one go*o*se, two ge*e*se) or terminal (I walk, he walk*s*); in some other languages, the internal or terminal inflections are far more numerous.

The inflection of nouns and pronouns is called *declension*; of verbs, *conjugation*; and of adjectives and adverbs, *comparison*. Conjunctions, prepositions, and interjections —which undergo no change—are called *uninflected* parts of speech.

Example of inflected verb: We *walked*; he *walks*. The *s* in *walks* indicates a change of person from first to third, a change of number from plural to singular, and a change of tense from past to present.

9.

INTERJECTION—a word or group of words grammatically independent of the sentence which conveys mild to strong emotion: *Oh*, please forget it. *Land sakes*, Huck! Sit down a mite. *Well!* That takes the cake!

A mild interjection is followed by a comma, a strong interjection by an exclamation point. Use sparingly.

9.

IRONY—from the Greek, *eironeia,* meaning "deception," "dissimulation"; the word has two general meanings:

1. as a figure of speech wherein the speaker says one thing but intends the opposite to be understood. In Shakespeare's *Julius Caesar,* there is irony in Mark Antony's speech to the citizens. They gradually realize that when he repeats that Brutus and the rest are "honorable men," he is speaking ironically (or sarcastically) and means exactly the opposite. When they fully perceive this, they cry: "They were traitors . . . villains, murderers." (Also called *verbal irony* or *rhetorical irony*.)

2. as *dramatic irony,* the use of language that has an inner significance or dimension unrecognized by some of the actors in a scene. In *Oedipus Rex,* when Oedipus speaks of the blindness of Tiresias with scorn, Tiresias and the audience know, but Oedipus does not, that he is soon to suffer blindness himself.

In certain poetic criticism and analysis, a poem is regarded as ironic if it is complex enough to take into account the incongruities and nuances of experience.

9.

ITALICS—When printed out, italics appear as a slightly slanted typeface. To indicate italics in handwriting or on an ordinary typewriter, you underline the word, phrase, or sentence. Three common uses follow:

1. Use italics for the titles of books, plays, and films. (Book: I read Richard Wright's *Native Son*.)

2. Italicize words used as words (or numbers used as numbers). As: *Jungle* and *kismet* are derived from Persian. Or: How many *7s* are there in 742677?

3. Italicize Latin abbreviations in footnotes of term papers, as *ibid., op. cit., passim*.

Use quotation marks, not italics, for individual short poems, short stories, and magazine articles.

Some other uses: foreign words not yet accepted as ordinary English, (as: *c'est la vie*); names of ships (as: the U.S.S. *Constitution*); words for emphasis (as: I said *his* house, not hers).

9.

ITS AND IT'S—*Its* is the possessive form of the pronoun *it* and requires no *apostrophe* (*which see*). *It's* is a contraction of *it is* and requires an apostrophe.

1. Each group must do *its* best. ("*Its*" possesses the word *best* and stands for "each group's.")

2. It's time to go. (*It's* is a contracted form of *it is*.) *Note:* The form *its'* does not exist.

10.

JARGON—the slang of a particular sport, profession, business, or group. Since it is highly specialized, the meaning of the words and phrases is often not clear or intelligible to the outsider. Unless the jargon itself is the subject of the paper, the careful writer should avoid this largely private diction. Examples: *sucker him in* or *providing the equalizer* from football; *bullish* and *bearish* from high finance, although such terms cross over into regular usage.

12.

LETTER—The model that follows will demonstrate a letter of application for a job or for information about a school.

Use regular 8½-by-11-inch typing paper. All business letters should be typed if at all possible. Be neat—clean paper, no erasures, no typing errors, no smudges.

The Heading

[your address & the date]   215 West 91st Street
New York, N. Y. 10024
August 29, 1975

Ms. Myra Speagle, Director   [person & company where
The Octagon Company   letter is going; if ad-
32 Broadway   dressee is a man, use Mr.]
New York, New York 10003

Dear Ms. Speagle: [note colon after name]

1st paragraph: the specific job you are applying for and how you learned of the opening.

2nd paragraph: information about yourself—background in school, degrees, special courses and training, specific experience, why you think you are suitable for the job, what you expect from it.

3rd paragraph: documents you will furnish—transcript of high school and college records, recommendations—followed by names and addresses of people who will supply references.

4th paragraph: request for an interview. (Be very firm in requesting an interview.)

Sincerely yours,
[full name signed]
Jessica Johnson

If the letter is addressed to a school for information, follow the same kind of heading and close. Sample heading: Registrar, The City College of New York, Convent Avenue & 138th Street, New York, N. Y. 10031. The first paragraph should state what information you wish—perhaps a catalogue, a special program, the names of particular faculty, fees and tuition costs, grant and scholarship applications, dates of school opening and holidays, etc. If you have complicated requests, more than one paragraph may be necessary. Do not run items together; be sure each request is clear and distinct, or else the answers may prove unsatisfactory or incomplete.

Envelope: In upper left-hand corner, put your name and address, blocked. Centered on envelope:

> Ms. Myra Speagle, Director
> The Octagon Company
> 32 Broadway
> New York, N. Y. 10003

12.

LIE, LAY—*Lie* means "rest," as: I want *to lie* down. I *lie* down every day. In the past tense: I *lay* down yesterday. In the perfect tense: I *have lain* down every day this week. *Lie* never takes a direct object.

Lay means "place" or "put," as: I *lay* the book on the table. In the past: I *laid* the problem to rest. In the perfect: I *have laid* the foundation for the house.

The progressive tense produces errors: I *was lying* down, not I *was laying* down; I *was laying* the table, not I *was lying* the table.

	lie	*lay*
Present:	lie	— lay
Past:	lay	— laid
Perfect:	lain	— laid
Progressive:	is lying	— is laying
Future:	will lie	— will lay

Lie is confused with *lay* because the present tense of *lay* is the same as the past tense of *lie*.

12.

LIKE (AS, AS IF)—*Like* is a preposition: *as* and *as if* are conjunctions. In formal English, write: She looks *as if* she hasn't any money, not, *like* she hasn't any money. Also: This stew tastes tart, *as* it should. Do not say: *like* it should.

12.

LOOSE SENTENCE—a sentence in which the main or principal clause (or statement) comes first, and the latter part contains subordinate or trailing elements. Example: The wedding we went to was very pleasant and I enjoyed the food [end of main element], but the idea of seeing the family was most interesting and I enjoyed the reception which followed and I won't forget it very soon, but . . . (After the main idea at the beginning, the sentence has no logical stopping point.) Try to write *periodic sentences* (*which see*).

13.

METAPHOR—a kind of figurative language; that is, language that departs from literal meaning to achieve special meaning or effect through implied comparison or analogy. In using metaphor, the writer finds similarities in dissimilar things or ideas. In *simile* (*which see*), a comparison between two essentially different things is expressed, through *like* or *as*. ("O my love is *like* a red, red rose.") In metaphor, the relationship of ideas or people or objects is made directly; metaphor can range far more broadly and adventurously than simile. A good example of metaphor, from Donne's "Holy Sonnet" No. 6: "Death be not proud, though some have called thee / Mighty and dreadful, for thou art not so."

Young writers often become entangled in metaphors. A combination of two metaphors whose literal meanings clash with each other yields a *mixed metaphor*, as in: My love, a red, red rose, tinkled with laughter. A rose obviously cannot tinkle. Such an error may be corrected if you suppress one of the metaphors, change one, or say literally what you mean: My love, a red, red bell, tinkled with laughter. A bell can tinkle.

In using metaphor, do not forget that you must honor its literal sense as well as its extended meanings.

METER—the pattern of a verse or line of poetry which is determined by the prevailing stress pattern and the number of such stress patterns (or feet). The commonest foot in English poetry is iambic: one unstressed and one stressed syllable, in that order, as in: today (tŏ dáy). There are also:

> trochaic   ╱ ∪
> anapestic   ∪ ∪ ╱
> dactyllic   ╱ ∪ ∪
> spondaic   ╱ ╱
> pyrrhic   ∪ ∪

The meter of the following line is, roughly, iambic pentameter: "To be, or not to be, that is the question . . . " (It consists of five feet of the iambic stress.)

If the line is made up of one foot, it is called *monometer;* of two, *dimeter;* of three, *trimeter;* of four, *tetrameter;* of five, *pentameter;* of six, *hexameter* (also called the *alexandrine*). Unrhymed iambic pentameter is *blank verse;* rhyming lines of iambic pentameter result in the *heroic couplet* (two successive lines). Determining the kind and number of feet in a line is called *scansion,* or *scanning the line. Free verse* (not to be confused with *blank verse*) has an *irregular metrical pattern* and substitutes cadences and rhythms for a uniform meter.

Warning: Do not confuse *meter* with *rhythm*. Rhythm is a totality of effects in poetry or prose; meter is only one element.

13.

MISPLACED ELEMENTS—words or phrases placed too distant from what they relate to. Whenever possible, words should be placed close to their natural positions: modifiers next to what they modify, direct objects after their verbs, verbs after their subjects, relative pronouns next to their antecedents. Here are some instances of misplaced elements:

1. The American people *despite the economic recession* have money in *most* of their pockets. (Read: Despite the economic recession, most American people have money in their pockets.)

2. Most of the Congress (*according to the President*) had *either* turned openly hostile or had become barely receptive to his new program. (According to the President, most of the Congress either had turned openly hostile . . .)

3. Hanging from a limb, Grandma saw a bird's nest. (This is an example of a dangling participle. Correct to: Grandma saw a bird's nest hanging from a limb.)

14.

NARRATIVE—Simply stated, a narrative is a story. It may be a parable, an anecdote, a short story, a novel, or even verse. If the narrative is a simple sequence of events, it is a *story;* if the narrative requires us to ask "Why did it happen?" rather than "What happened next?" we have a story with *plot* (*which see*).

In traditional rhetoric, the other forms of writing are *description, exposition,* and *argumentation* (*see all*).

14.

NONE—Grammarians often insist that *none* must always be singular on the grounds that it stems from *not one*, but it may take a plural verb when the sense implies more than one.

1. None of their things *are* among them. (*None* implies several.) but:

2. None of them *is* the man. (*None* is clearly a single unit.)

If the plural verb is used after *none*, the possessive pronoun that follows must be plural: None of the students *have* taken *their* examinations.

14.

NON SEQUITUR—meaning, "it does not follow." A non sequitur occurs when elements do not follow each other logically (or when conclusions do not follow from premises). Example: Since George is a religious person, we did not expect him to commit that terrible crime. (The conclusion is drawn that religious people will not commit crimes.)

14.

NOUN—a word that names a person, place, thing, substance, quality, idea, action, or state of being. In English, the noun changes only in the plural (by adding an *s*, as in *clock, clocks,* or by a stem change, as in *man, men*). The student uncertain of identifying nouns should test them by putting *a* or *an* before them: *a sound, an assist, a party.* These make sense. The following do not: *an if, a pretty, an attacking.*

NUMBER (SINGULAR AND PLURAL)—English requires agreement in number of parts of a sentence, especially subject and verb. When the sense of the subject is singular, the verb is singular, irrespective of its position:

1. *One* of the visitors *has* left.
2. The *number* of cars on the highway *is* amazing.

A plural subject when it signifies a single or mass concept may take a singular verb:

1. The *power and the glory is* forever.
2. The *United States has* a large population.

The difficulty arises when the subject is removed from the verb, or is compound (more than one). If the writer keeps in mind what his subject is, the difficulty is lessened:

1. This *account* of France's music art, literature, and sports *gives* the reader a full picture. (Singular subject and singular verb.)
2. Hemingway wrote the sort of *books which,* he thought, *were* what the public wanted. (*Which* is subject of the verb *were,* and *which* refers to *books,* a plural form—that makes everything plural.)
3. The long opening *paragraph* of the novel and the rather short *chapter* in which it appears *have* puzzled some critics. (*Paragraph* and *chapter* form the compound subject of *have.*)
4. The *heart* and *mind* of man *are* unconquerable. (*Heart* and *mind* from the compound subject of *are; man* has no bearing on the verb.)

15.

OBJECT (DIRECT, INDIRECT, OBJECT OF PREPOSITION)—A *direct object* is a noun or noun equivalent toward which the action of the verb is directed. The direct object answers the question: What? or Whom? It *never* comes after any form of the verb *to be* (*was, am, are, is,* etc). The verb *to be* takes a *predicate adjective* or a *predicate noun* (*nominative*). In the sentence "Mary is a *doctor*," doctor is not an object, but a predicate noun or predicate nominative. In the sentence "John is *tall*," tall is a predicate adjective.

Normally, the direct object of the verb is placed right after the verb (allowing for adjectives):

1. He danced the *Latin American number* fast. (He danced what?)

2. I saw my *friend Helen* in the distance. (I saw whom?)

The *indirect object* rarely creates any problems in writing, except when the indirect object is a pronoun. An indirect object answers the question: to whom? or for whom?

1. He gave [to] *me* the gift. (Or: He gave the gift to me.) If the indirect object is a pronoun, be sure it is an object pronoun (*me, him, them, her,* etc.).

The *object of the preposition* is the noun or pronoun, or noun equivalent, after a preposition:

1. He came home on the *train*. (Object of *on*.)

2. She went to the *picnic* with her closest *friends*. (Object of *to;* object of *with*.)

The object plus its preposition (*to the picnic, on the train*) is a *prepositional phrase*.

15.

OTHER (OTHERWISE)—as an adjective, *other* assumes parallel ideas in the same category as that implied by what has been said. Examples:

1. Into the soup went onions, carrots, lentils, okra, and several *other* vegetables. (*Other* is used correctly because all the ingredients are vegetables.)

2. During his freshman year, he studied sex education, economics, social reform, urban planning, and several *other* problems. (*Other* is used incorrectly because the list of items is not solely of problems.)

15.

OUTLINE—*See under* COMPOSITION.

16.

PARADOX—a statement which, though apparently self-contradictory, contains a basis of truth. A paradox conflicts with received opinion or belief and often provokes the reader to consider the particular point of view afresh, as when Shakespeare says, "Cowards die many times before their deaths"; and Wordsworth, "The Child is father of the Man."

16.

PARALLELISM—the use of similar constructions for similar concepts. In a sentence, the words, phrases, and clauses that are equal in thought should be equal grammatically. Some examples and their types:

1. *Jack* and *Jill* went up the hill. (Parallel nouns for subject.)

2. He drinks *coffee, tea,* and *milk.* (Parallel nouns for direct objects.)

3. We shall fight them *on the sea, in the air, on the beaches, in the towns, fields,* and *cities.* (Parallel nouns as objects of prepositions *in* and *on.*)

4. The purpose of this book is *to clarify expression* and *to improve communication.* (Parallel infinitives.)

5. *Slashing forward through the line, swerving past the safety man, sprinting like a gazelle,* he scored the winning touchdown. (Parallel participles and participial phrases.)

6. Gandhi was a man *who believed in nonviolence, who revered all life,* and *who resisted the English passively.* (Parallel subordinate clauses.)

Remember: once you begin a particular kind of construction in a series of items, continue that type of construction.

16.

PARENTHESES—Parentheses (singular: parenthesis) are used to enclose information not vital to the thought but related to it. Parentheses should not be used when the material is important, nor should the wording within the parentheses be part of the grammatical structure of the sentence outside. Correct usages:

1. A very short summing-up at the end of the essay (if one is necessary) is better left as a separate paragraph.

2. The second volume of his memoirs (the first was published last year) should appear in translation in 1980.

Parenthetical material often appears between commas or dashes instead of parentheses.

16.

PARODY—a literary caricature which mimics the themes and style (or tone and manner) of some other author or person so that his faults seem absurd and laughable. The method is usually exaggeration. *See also* SATIRE.

16.

PARTICIPIAL PHRASE—the participle plus whatever words go with it, as in: *Seeing the accident occur before his eyes,* he ran for the police. Or: *Having weak eyesight,* she needed guidance. The word after the participial phrase must make sense with the phrase. *Seeing* goes with *he; having* goes with *she.*

16.

PARTICIPLE—A participle looks like a verb (without being a verb) and serves as an adjective; it is, therefore, called a *verbal adjective*. It is formed by adding *-ed* or *-ing* (sometimes *-en*) to the stem of the verb. As an adjective, the participle modifies or describes someone or something; as a verb, it may take an object. Examples:

1. Striking the boy, the car plunged on. (*Striking* is the participle: it comes from the verb *strike* and it modifies *car*. It also happens to have a direct object, *boy*.)

2. Shaken by the news, he nearly collapsed. (*Shaken* is the participle: it comes from the verb *shake* and it modifies *he*. There is no object here.)

Avoid the *dangling participle*. This error occurs when a participle is not firmly attached to the only word it can correctly modify. Examples:

1. Being small, I knew everyone in my college. (The participle *being* actually modifies *I* when it surely is meant to refer to *college*. Correct: Because my college is small, I knew everyone.)

2. While reading the second act of *Hamlet*, Shakespeare comes to life. (Probably this means: While I was reading the second act of *Hamlet*, Shakespeare came to life for me.)

16.

PARTS OF SPEECH—the eight categories by which words are classified according to the function they perform in a sentence: *noun, pronoun, verb, adjective, adverb, preposition, conjunction, interjection (see all)*. Though the dictionary lists the parts of speech a word may be, it is more logical to determine what part of speech a word is by the function it performs in a given sentence. Many words can be used as several parts of speech:

1. Ali predicted a knockout in the first *round*. (As noun.)
2. It is a *round object*. (As adjective.)
3. She'll be coming *round* the mountain. (As preposition.)
4. They *round* the bend at high speed. (As verb.)
5. Don't fool *'round*. (As adverb.)

In general, words are *nouns* and *pronouns* when they name persons, places, things, ideas, or states of being; *verbs* when they express action or a state of being; *adjectives* and *adverbs* when they modify or describe; *prepositions* when they show connections; *conjunctions* when they join clauses; and *interjections* when they convey emotion.

16.

PERIODIC SENTENCE—a sentence in which the reader cannot complete his understanding of the thought until he reaches the last word. Such sentences require more planning as a rule than the *loose sentence* (*which see*), but in compensation they enable the writer to hold the reader's attention until the very end. Overdone, the periodic sentence may become artificial and overcontrived. Here are some good examples:

1. England expects every man to do his duty.
2. Give me liberty or give me death.
3. He who fights too long with the dragon becomes like the dragon.

16.

PHRASE—A phrase is a group of words that does not have a subject *and* a verb; it may contain a verb form or a word that looks like a subject, *but it cannot contain both*. If it did contain both, it would be a clause, not a phrase. There are several kinds of phrases, and they must never be used as if they were complete thoughts. *The writer's failure to distinguish between phrases and clauses leads to sentence fragments.* The main types are:

Prepositional phrase: I am going *to the store for a loaf of bread.* (A prepositional phrase is introduced by a preposition, which is followed by a noun or pronoun. That noun or pronoun is the object of the preposition. There are three such phrases in the example.)

Infinitive phrase: I wish *to try out my new fishing rod.* (An infinitive phrase begins with an infinitive and includes whatever material goes with it. *To try out* is the infinitive; *my new fishing rod* is the object of the infinitive.)

Participial phrase: Having studied hard, she passed the examination. (A participial phrase is introduced by a participle—here, *having studied*—and includes whatever goes with the participle—here, the word *hard.*)

Gerund phrase: Walking to the camp site is hard work. (A gerund phrase is introduced by a gerund—here, *walking*—and includes whatever goes with the gerund—here, *to the camp site.* The gerund *walking* is subject of the verb *is.*) A gerund phrase may be object of the verb: I liked *winning the game.* A gerund phrase may also be object of a preposition: I am fond of *winning all my bets.*

Remember, if a phrase does not fit into one of these types, it is probably not a phrase—it may be a clause or it may be just an odd group of words.

16.

PLAGIARISM—Whenever a writer uses the exact words and phrasing of another writer without acknowledgment, he is guilty of *plagiarism*. Plagiarism occurs most frequently on term papers, where the student, afraid that he cannot handle the language and the mechanics of documentation, simply appropriates the material he is consulting as his own. There is a simple and perfectly acceptable way to avoid plagiarism—put *quotation marks* (*which see*) around any phrase or sentence of more than five words you are taking from your source; then footnote the borrowing. Another way to handle the material is to paraphrase it—put the statement into your own language and *footnote the idea*. General ideas, of course, are in the public domain, and even if you encounter the idea in your reading, you are not expected to cite the specific source.

16.

PLOT—a group of chronologically ordered events that are also related to one another by cause and effect. The plot of a play or novel may not be readily apparent: events may be related out of sequence and the effect one event has upon another may not be obvious. However, if a work of literature is to be considered successful, it must be *more* than a haphazard arrangement of events, *even if it seems haphazard.*

16.

POINT OF VIEW—the position from which the writer considers or evaluates his subject. The point of view should remain consistent throughout the work (essay, story, poem, drama, novel). In *Aspects of the Novel,* E. M. Forster summed up some examples of point of view: "The novel can either describe the characters from outside, as an impartial or partial onlooker; or he can assume omniscience and describe them from within; or he can place himself in the position of one of them and affect to be in the dark as to the motives of the rest; or there are certain intermediate attitudes." Because of "point of view," the reader should not identify the author of a novel or a play with any one of his characters or with any single event.

16.

PREPOSITION—the part of speech that connects nouns and pronouns to other parts of the sentence. Common prepositions are: *on, in, into, among, between, within, over, beyond, to, with*. He walked *into* the room. *Into* is a preposition, and *into the room* is a prepositional phrase.

PRONOUN—a word that takes the place of a noun or noun concept. There are several kinds of pronouns:

Personal: I, you, he, she, it, we, they, me, him, her, them

Possessive: my, mine, your, yours, his, her, hers, its, our, ours, their, theirs

Demonstrative: this, these, that, those

Relative: who, whom, which, that

Reflexive: myself, yourself, herself, himself, itself, themselves

Most difficulties with pronouns occur with agreement and reference. A pronoun must agree with its antecedent (or the word it replaces). Examples:

1. The group leaves for California tomorrow. *They* have ten days of vacation. (*Group* is singular here; *they have* should be *it has.*)

2. John picked up his hat. Mary picked up *hers,* but her sisters left theirs. (*Hers* agrees in gender with Mary; *theirs* agrees in number with *sisters.*) *Note:* There is no apostrophe in *hers* or *theirs*—these words are already possessive forms.

Sometimes a pronoun is used to refer to an idea; this is faulty usage. The pronoun should refer to a single word. Example: I would like to be a teacher, but it is a crowded field. (*It* has no referent; the implied antecedent is *teaching,* not *teacher.*) Change to: Teaching is a crowded field, but I would still like to be a teacher.

Who is a subject word; *whom* is an object word:

1. He is a man *who* will go far. (*Who* is used as subject of the verb *go.*)

2. He is a man *who* I think is generous.

3. This is a person for *whom* I have little use. (*Whom* is used as object of the preposition *for.*)

Use *who* and *whom* for persons; use *that* and *which* for objects and animals.

129

16.

PROTAGONIST—the chief character in a play or other work of fiction, from the Greek *protagonistes,* meaning the first actor in a drama. In Sophocles' *Antigone,* there are two protagonists, Antigone and Creon. In Arthur Miller's *Death of a Salesman,* the protagonist is Willy Loman.

17.

PUNCTUATION—a number of marks which help the writer to convey his exact meaning; they also aid the reader to understand what is before him. Punctuation is not arbitrary, and it is not based on breath control. *See* APOSTROPHE; COLON; COMMA; DASH; HYPHEN; QUOTATION MARKS; SEMICOLON.

17.

QUESTION MARK—used chiefly after a direct question as: Did Cromwell really kill a king? Caution: Do not use a question mark after an indirect question, as: She asked John where he got hold of the book.

Also, use a question mark to indicate a doubtful or approximate statement, as with dates: the Hundred Years War (1337?–1453).

18.

QUOTATION MARKS—These have two chief uses, in direct quotation and to punctuate different kinds of published material.

1. John said, "I will arrive at three, on Wednesday." (Direct quotation.)

2. "Shall I compare thee to a Summer's day?" is the opening line of Shakespeare's Sonnet No. 18. (Direct quotation.)

3. "The Antheap" is a story from Doris Lessing's *African Stories*. (Punctuation around a story title.) Also use quotation marks around the titles of poems, essays, and magazine articles.

Sometimes *quotation marks* are found around words or phrases used ironically or used as slang. *Avoid* overuse of this.

1. Although he is a reactionary, he calls himself a "liberal." (Irony.)

2. Don't try to "turn me on." (Slang.)

Sometimes you will see single quotation marks. This occurs in English usage or in American usage when a quote is placed within a quote: In one of his essays, Thomas Mann writes, "We must heed the words of Dostoevsky: 'Honor life before the meaning of life.' "

18.

REAL—Do not use *real* in place of *really* or *very*. Do not say: This is *real* good, but: This is *really* good, or: This is *very* good.

18.

REALISM—a term that has application to literature, philosophy, aesthetics, and everyday life. In its commonest meaning, realism is a fidelity to facts as these facts are perceived by the senses and by experience. Realism assumes that the universe actually exists as we see it, and is not a creation of the mind or understanding. As a literary movement, realism flourished in the 19th century as a reaction against the excesses of sentimentality and romanticism. Some of the chief realist writers were Tolstoy, George Eliot, Thackeray, Jane Austen, some of the works of Dickens, Crane, Howells, Henry James, Balzac, and Flaubert.

18.

REASON—Many people say: The reason is *because*. . . . The correct usage is: The reason is *that*. *Reason* and *that* should be parallel parts of speech: The reason for his absence is *that* he didn't feel well. Or, reworded: Because he didn't feel well, he was absent.

18.

REDUNDANT OR REPETITIOUS—means that the writer has said the same thing more than once, as in: Some of the courses at college are interesting, but not all of them. *But not all of them* is implied by the first part of the sentence and should be eliminated. There are occasions when you may want to repeat a word, phrase, or idea for *emphasis,* but that is quite different from repetition that has no function and arises from carelessness. Redundancy is a serious writing fault.

RESEARCH PAPER—Also called a *library paper* or *term paper*, this is a piece of work usually running from 1,500 to 2,000 words, although length may vary. For development of a research paper, *see* COMPOSITION; a research or library paper has the same development as the shorter composition. The chief differences are that for the research paper you need a more extensive topic and must use library materials.

1. *Choose your topic.* Make sure your topic will be broad enough for the required length, but not too broad. Perhaps you are interested in crime and its prevention. Do not select the entire field, which requires a book. Choose an aspect—possibly how better schooling of the child leads to a lower crime rate, or how better housing for individuals of all ages reduces the crime rate. Or you may start with such assumptions, only to discover that better schooling and housing do *not* reduce the rate of crime. Your investigation of the material, in which you discover something you did not know before, could be the content of your research paper.

2. *Make an informal outline* of what you plan to do, what will be included, what basic points you will be stressing. If your instructor requires a formal outline, then he will tell you. (*See* end of this entry for a formal outline.) Probably he will leave that to you. Work from a sketch, a list of items, or a set of headings. The outline will provide direction and focus.

3. *Check the card catalog* at your school and town library for information about your subject. Select three or four books and some magazine articles (from *Reader's Guide to Periodical Literature, Ulrich's Periodical Directory,* or *The New York Times Index*). Get their authors and titles correct; put them on index cards or sheets of paper.

4. *Go through the library material,* copying out passages or ideas you may want to use. Collect more information than you will use, since you cannot tell yet what you will include. Copy accurately—be certain of that. Take down page numbers, or else you will have to retrace your steps. If you take care the first time through, you can avoid a good deal of time-consuming rechecking.

In addition to the guides listed above, the following may be useful:

Encyclopedia Britannica and *Encyclopedia Americana*
Dictionary of American Biography and *Dictionary of National Biography* (English)
An Encyclopedia of World History
Dictionary of World Literature
Dictionary of Philosophy and Psychology and *Encyclopedia of Psychology*
Encyclopedia of the Social Sciences
Technical and Scientific Encyclopedia
Social Work Yearbook

Further, you should ask your librarian for information and help or consult the *Guide to Reference Books* (published by the American Library Association).

5. *The list of books* you use is called your *bibliography.* Entries appear alphabetized by author at the end of your research paper. Entries look like this:

Menninger, Karl. *Modern Prisons.* New York: Random House, 1963. [book entry]
Newcomb, George. "Do Our Schools Work?" *Harpers Magazine,* XC (August 1965), 362–374. [magazine entry; XC is volume number]
"Prisons," *Encyclopedia Britannica,* 14th edition, XV, 642–721. [encyclopedia article; note that entry is alphabetized by title, since there is no author]

Remember: Alphabetize each item, whether a book, article, poem, or short story.

6. *When you begin to write,* follow the same principles of development that you would for a shorter composition. Give yourself a topic sentence or two; build up your paragraphs; make sure you have transitions from paragraph to paragraph.

7. *Footnoting* is necessary to show the sources of your information. Be very accurate, and keep your footnoting technique simple. You lead the reader to your footnote by means of a number next to a word in the text, as this indicates [1]—that number may lead to a reference or to a further idea. Put footnotes at the bottom of the page on which they occur in the text, or in consecutive order just before your bibliography. Number them consecutively: 1, 2, 3, etc. The reference will look like this:

1 Menninger, *Modern Prisons,* p. 47.
2 Newcomb, "Do Our Schools Work?" p. 368.
3 "Prisons," *Encyclopedia Britannica,* p. 643.

Note: the reference is simple, since complete information on each book appears in the bibliography. If you paraphrase an idea that is not your own, then provide a source for it. You can do that by writing "As Menninger points out . . . " In that way, you can avoid the footnote for an idea.

8. *Forget* about *ibid., op. cit., loc. cit., passim*—unless your instructor wants to see your use of these traditional terms. They are disappearing, however, and are being replaced by a shorthand reference to the source, such as: Menninger, p. 17.

9. *When you have finished your first draft,* place all the footnoted material in order. Then revise the text several times—both wording and organization.

10. *Reread* the finished product. Do not give it to someone else to type and proofread. Give yourself time to relax before rereading and correcting.

If your instructor wants a formal outline, it looks like this: Thesis or topic sentence indicating your plan. Then:

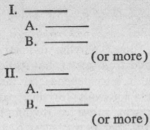

I. ——
   A. ——
   B. ——
         (or more)
II. ——
   A. ——
   B. ——
         (or more)

And so on until you have covered your material. A paper of 1,500–2,000 words may have 20–25 paragraphs. Your Roman numerals in the outline should each stand for several paragraphs. *See also* COMPOSITION for form of outline.

18.

RHYTHM—the measured flow of words and phrases in verse or prose, from the Greek *rhythmos,* meaning "measured motion" or "flow." Rhythm in poetry is quite different from rhyme and from meter, but its flow is connected to both of them; it also depends on the recurrence of sounds and on the intervals (or time passage) between sounds. In its own way, prose has rhythm, less pronounced than that of poetry, but nevertheless tied to sounds, intervals, and recurrences.

18.

RUN-ON SENTENCE—This error, also called *fused* or *run-together sentence,* occurs when two main (independent) clauses are not separated by any punctuation at all. These two main clauses should be joined by a coordinating conjunction, or separated by a semicolon, colon, or period— whichever is appropriate. Example: The ignition was turned on the motor coughed. (A run-on sentence.) The following corrections are all possible: The ignition was turned on, *and* the motor coughed. The ignition was turned on; the motor coughed. The ignition was turned on. The motor coughed. *When* the ignition was turned on, the motor coughed. (The final version is best, since it indicates cause and effect.)

The error is a bad one and can usually be avoided if you distinguish between main and subordinate clauses. Words like *however, consequently, thus, that is, moreover,* and *nevertheless* do not subordinate a clause; whereas words like *when, that, who, since, unless, because,* and *although* do subordinate a clause. If you have main clauses, you must provide the joining or separation indicated above—a full stop (semicolon or period), or a coordinating conjunction with a comma, or a subordinating conjunction for one of the clauses. (*See* CONJUNCTION.) The following sentences are correct: He worked hard at revision; consequently, his papers improved. He worked hard at revision; his papers improved, consequently. Because he worked hard at revision, his papers improved. He worked hard at revision. His papers improved. (The last is correct, but made up of baby sentences.)

(*See* COMMA SPLICE.)

19.

SATIRE—a literary device which submits vice or folly or stupidity to ridicule and mockery, often making use of *irony* (*which see*) and *sarcasm*. Some examples of literary satire are Swift's *Gulliver's Travels* and *A Modest Proposal*, Orwell's *1984*, Byron's *Don Juan*, and Heller's *Catch-22*. Swift said: "Satire is a sort of glass wherein beholders do generally discover everybody's face but their own."

19.

SEMICOLON—used chiefly to separate independent clauses; it resembles the period in this usage, but carries the suggestion that the clauses are more closely connected in meaning than those separated by a period. As: His first film was enormously impressive; his second had less impact.

Avoid use of the semicolon when comma, dash, or colon is called for. As: That decision brings him to the most perilous moment of his life; facing the guns of the enemy. (The semicolon should be a colon, or even a dash.)

One other use: to separate groups that already contain elements separated by commas. For example: At the party were: John, a printer; Alice, a potter; Mary, a policewoman; and Joe, a mechanic.

SENTENCE VARIETY AND SENTENCE KINDS—A writer should vary the length, pattern, and kind of sentences he uses, to avoid dullness and repetition. Short sentences throughout a paper create a choppy effect, while long, smoothly flowing sentences can act as a drug. Either of these effects may be appropriate on occasion, but as a rule the writer should try different lengths until he finds what is natural for him. *The best sentence is the one that gives the right emphasis.*

The *simple sentence* consists of one main clause only:
1. Time flies.
2. He left for the station in the morning.
3. Stop! ("You" is understood as the subject.)
4. John and Mary could not arrive on time. (Compound subject, but only one main clause.)

The *compound sentence* contains more than one main clause, but no subordinate clause:
1. Men screamed and women wept.
2. I wanted to register early, but my train was late.
3. Temperatures sometimes dip to freezing, and sometimes there are snowfalls heavy enough to block the mountain passes; but, generally, the climate is very equitable.

In a compound sentence, three main clauses, as in 3 above, may seem excessive, although correct.

The *complex sentence* contains one main clause and *at least one* (and perhaps more than one) subordinate clause:
1. They ran when the gun went off. (*When the gun went off* is the subordinate clause.)
2. The gun that went off frightened them. (*That went off* is the subordinate clause.)
3. We heard that a gun had been fired. (*That a gun had been fired* is the subordinate clause.)

4. If you like, take the car. (*If you like* is the subordinate clause.)

The *compound-complex sentence:* combines compound and complex sentences, so that it consists of more than one main clause and at least one subordinate clause: He knew what to do, but he had forgotten to bring the tools that he needed. (Two main clauses and one subordinate clause.)

See also CLAUSE for information on main and subordinate clauses. You cannot work on sentence variety unless you understand the structure of your sentences.

19.

SENTIMENTAL, SENTIMENTALISM, SENTIMENTALITY
—These words indicate excessive emotion for the given situation in a story, novel, play, or dramatic poem. *Sentiment* is not to be confused with *sentimentality;* the latter is an overindulgence in emotion or emotional situations and often leads to melodrama. Such overindulgence can be found in "purple" prose, fainting heroines, soft-hearted characters, the "pure prostitute." As a literary school, sentimentalism began in the 18th century in the drama and in the novel (*Pamela, The Vicar of Wakefield, Tristram Shandy, The Man of Feeling*). A good modern example is Erich Segal's *Love Story,* both the novel and the motion picture based upon it.

19.

SEQUENCE OF TENSES—Time sequences of the verb should be similar or consistent when you go between main and subordinate elements. Often the meaning intended dictates the necessary sequences. Examples:

1. I *shake* his hand because I *respect* his integrity. (Both verbs in the present tense.)

2. I *shook* his hand because I *respected* his integrity. (Both verbs in past—the situation is finished.)

3. I *shook* his hand because I *respect* his integrity. (Past tense of verb in the main clause, present tense in the subordinate clause showing habitual action—I still respect him.)

4. After we *discussed* the matter thoroughly, we *agreed* that she is the best choice for the deanship, and we *hope* that she *will be released* by her department. (Past action before the present decision.)

5. I *will oppose* him because I now *realize* that we *have been misled* for six years. (Future action motivated by a present awareness [*realize*] based upon an action extending from the past into the present—*have been misled*.)

For the *infinitive* (*which see*), the sequence of tenses involves two principles: the present infinitive always expresses action at the same time as the action of the main verb; and second, the perfect infinitive expresses action prior to the main action:

1. He *plays* the piano *to relax*. (Same time.)

2. He *played* the piano *to relax*. (Same time.)

3. He *will play* the piano *to relax*. (Same time.)

4. He *is known to have played* the piano. (Prior action.)

5. We *are sorry to have missed his playing*. (Prior action.)

Caution: If you tell a story or relate an episode, *decide on a tense* (past, present, future) and *stick to it. The present is usually more vivid.*

SHIFT OF VOICE, MOOD, TENSE, PERSON, NUMBER—
At times a sentence heads in one direction, then shifts to
another. Often this shift happens because the writer for-
gets that he has started with one mood, tense, number,
person, or voice and has changed to another. (*See also*
PARALLELISM.) Some examples of these shifts follow:
1. Books require special care so that *it* does not disinte-
grate. (Shift in number—use *they.*)
2. The Concrete Poets take pleasure in graphic design,
and meaning *is* usually *subordinated* to form. (Shift in
voice from active to passive—use *and they usually subordinate meaning to form.*)
3. They must listen, and *it* is important to listen carefully.
(Shift from personal *they* to impersonal *it*—use *and
listen carefully.*)
4. If you were I and I *was* you. (Shift in mood—use *I
were you,* in the subjunctive.)
5. Obey his orders and *we* will be safe. (Shift in person—
use *and you will be safe,* keeping both verbs as impera-
tives.)
6. Hemingway was an important American novelist; he
has written The Sun Also Rises about the Lost Genera-
tion. (Shift in tense—use *he wrote . . .*)

19.

SIC—literally, "thus." *Sic* (always italicized and in brackets) is used commonly when quoting after misspellings or other violations of strictly correct English: *sic* indicates to the reader that the mistake was in the original and not the fault of the writer quoting the material. Example: John wrote, "Hemmingway [*sic*] was a great author."

19.

SIMILE—a figure of speech that makes a comparison, pointing out a similarity between things otherwise unlike, for purposes of explanation, *allusion* (*which see*), or ornament. It is introduced by a word such as *like, as* or *such*. It can be simple, briefly expressed, or long and sustained, known then as the *epic simile*. Example: "Men fear death as children fear to go in the dark." (Francis Bacon) The simple simile is *as children fear to go in the dark.*

A *metaphor* (*which see*) makes the comparison directly, without the intervention of *as, like,* or *such.*

19.

SINCE, AS, BECAUSE—all three are commonly used to mean *the reason that*. In this sense, *as* is weak, *since* is acceptable, *because* is preferable. Note these examples:

1. *As* it was raining, I opened my umbrella. (Does this mean: Because it was raining? or During the time it was raining? Probably: *Because* it was raining . . .)
2. *Since* I was on the desert road, I was thirsty, hungry, and tired. (Probably: *Because* I was on the desert road . . .)

Since should be used to mean duration of time from a given starting point up to the present:

1. *Since* the beginning of civilization, men have waged war.
2. We have known each other *since* childhood.

As means "at that time," "when something is happening": The story broke *as* the paper was going to press.

19.

SPELLING—Because English orthography (the written language) has not been able to change as the spoken language has changed, spelling is difficult and inconsistent for many people. One can learn many rules, or one can study lengthy word lists of commonly misspelled words. We believe that anyone with a spelling problem would do better to consult his dictionary for every word over one or two syllables. This is time-consuming but there are no simple cures. *Remember:* If you do not find the word in the dictionary, do *not* go ahead and use that word. If you cannot find it, you are misspelling it to begin with.

19.

STORY—a group of events related to one another by time. Unlike the events of a *plot* (*which see*), the events of a story do not have a cause-and-effect relationship. The effect that one episode of a story has upon another is not significant. A story is "how things occur"; whereas a plot imposes a plan upon the elements of the story.

19.

STYLE—a way of writing or a mode of expression characteristic of an individual, or a literary school, a historical period, a nation (for example, difficult or easy style, classic style, Romanesque style, Shavian style, romantic style, etc.). It can also refer to the custom or plan followed in spelling, punctuation, and mechanics—what is called *stylistics*.

Any writing style works if it makes statements, rouses emotions, and puts facts with clarity and brevity, and does so with grace and cogency. No writing style can be effective unless it has content, organization, and direction. The following is a good stylistic checklist for you:

1. Does your writing have a point or direction?
2. Do you understand every word you are using?
3. Have you worked out the organization?
4. Are you using words for direct communication, not to impress the reader?
5. Have you eliminated repetition?
6. Have you avoided clichés or stereotyped words and phrases?
7. Have you used big words when small ones will do?
8. Do you have sentence variety?
9. Is there a logical sequence to your work?
10. Are your stylistics (mechanics) correct?

19.

SUBJECT—a noun, pronoun, or noun group about which something is said. Every sentence to be complete must have a subject. Usually, it comes first, but not always. Example:
1. The *weather* in Paris turns warm in May. (Subject first.)
2. In Paris, the *weather* turns warm in May. (Subject later.)
3. In Paris, in May, the *weather* turns warm. (Still later.)
4. Turning and shifting in the wind is my brother's *kite*. (Subject at end.)
5. In having Open Admissions at a large urban university does not prove anything yet. (This has no subject at all— it is a sentence fragment; leave out *in* and then *having* becomes the subject.) *Remember:* A noun or pronoun after a preposition cannot be the subject.

19.

SUBJUNCTIVE—Though the subjunctive mood of the verb is dying out of English, there are two uses of it still very much alive:

In sentences expressing a wish or a possibility contrary to fact:

1. I wish I *were* a pair of ragged claws. (Not *was* but *were* after the verb *wish*.)
2. If I *were* you, I would go. (Not *was* but *were* to express the contrary-to-fact situation.)

With verbs of request and command:

1. I move that the meeting *be* adjourned. (Not *is*.)
2. He asked that she *give* him a lift. (Not *gives*.)
3. The petition requested that the husband *pay* a weekly alimony. (Not *pays*.)

19.

SUBSTANTIVE—any word or combination of words that performs the grammatical function of a noun. A substantive may be a noun or any equivalent of a noun, such as a pronoun, an infinitive, a gerund, or a clause.

1. The *book* was heavy. (Noun as substantive.)
2. *He* thought *she* should go. (Pronouns as substantives.)
3. He wants *to leave*. (Infinitive as substantive, used as direct object of the verb.)
4. *Swimming* is a strenuous sport. (Gerund as substantive, subject of the sentence.)
5. We have not been told *why we are here*. (Noun clause as substantive, used as direct object of the verb.)

19.

SYMBOL—something that stands for an element (object, idea, person) not present. The cross is a symbol; so is the hammer and sickle. Some literary symbols are: in *The Great Gatsby,* the eye on the signboard, as well as the green lights; sun, moon, tower, and tree in the poetry of Yeats; the idea of the mountain in Mann's *Magic Mountain.* As R. G. Haggar puts it: "Symbols may be of many kinds: hieroglyphics, initials, emblems, allegories, fables, and (as in some modern art) enigmas. Some symbols closely approximate an idea or person and are easily recognized; others can be understood only by following some out-of-the-way association of ideas."

SYMBOLISM—the name of a school of 19th-century French poets which includes Baudelaire, Rimbaud, Verlaine, and Mallarmé, who aimed at presenting ideas and emotions through suggestion rather than by direct expression. They set symbolic meaning on objects, words, and sounds and as extreme individuals rebelled against *naturalism* and *realism* (*which see*).

19.

SYNECDOCHE—a figure of speech in which a part or a piece stands for the whole. For instance, we say: Xerxes attacked Greece with a thousand sail. We use *sail* for "ship," the part for the whole, and in this case the singular for the plural as well. *A thousand sail* means "a thousand ships." Used with caution synecdoche is an excellent way to make vague or ordinary writing more concrete.

19.

SYNTAX—the arrangement and grammatical relationship of words as parts of a sentence. A common synonym for syntax is *sentence construction*. In the sentence "I saw him at the store," the syntax is as follows:

I is the subject of the sentence.

Saw is the verb.

Him is the direct object of the verb *saw*.

At the store is a prepositional phrase used as an adverb because it modifies the verb *saw* (it answers the question "Where?").

Store is the object of the preposition *at*.

TENSE—a verb form that expresses distinctions of time. This entry covers only the principal tenses and errors.

Present tense: mainly for events or conditions at the time of writing or speaking.

1. She *likes* dancing. (Note the *s* on *likes,* present tense, third person singular form.)

2. He *contends* that he never saw her before. (*Saw* or *has seen* occurred before *he contends.*)

3. We *leave* for Rome tomorrow. (Use of present tense with a future idea.)

A frequent error connected with the present tense is using the past tense for the present: Making the basketball team means staying in shape and finding a position I *was* good at. (Correct: I *am* good at.) They discovered that copper *became* harder when it was mixed with tin. (It should be: *becomes* harder. This is a general truth; it always becomes harder.) In Book I, Gulliver is too large; in Book II, he *was* too small. (Correct: *is* too small.) *Note:* The events described in literary works or the techniques used by the author in expressing his material are never past. We cannot say that they *happened,* for they *happen* each time we read the book. Always discuss what is occurring in a literary work in the present tense. On the other hand, if you are discussing the relation of the work to the circumstances of the author's life or times, use the *past* tense: Swift *wrote* this book as a satire on the complacent English society of his time.

Present perfect tense: for situations and recurrent events that extend over a certain span of time up to and including the present.

1. She *has read* two of Bellow's novels. (A span of time.)

2. They *have been married* for five years. (Still married.)

A frequent error connected with the present perfect is using the present tense for the present perfect: Throughout history, men and women *try* to lead the poor to greater freedom. (Correct: *have tried,* to include action begun in past and continuing into the present.) I believe that *Portnoy's Complaint is* a financially successful novel. (Correct: *has been* or *was.*)

Past tense: for events and situations completed, done with, no matter how long ago; also called the *simple past.*
1. The 13 colonies *declared* their independence in 1776.
2. He *held* his breath for a minute. (But: He *has held* his breath for a minute now. This would indicate action continuing into the present.)

Frequent errors connected with the past tense are using the past for the present perfect and using the present perfect for the past: Many parents *permitted* their children to watch violent and superficial television shows. (Correct: *have permitted,* to indicate a continuing situation.) As an adult, I realize that many aspects of my adolescence *have been influenced* by our social mores. (Correct: *were influenced,* the simple past to indicate that adolescence is over for the writer.)

Past perfect tense: for a past prior to another specified past. I *had been studying* for about an hour when the telephone rang. (*Had* indicates a deeper past than *rang.*) *Note:* Distinctions of simple past and earlier past are necessary for sense. As: When he *decided* to leave for college, I felt he *found* himself. (Correct: *had found himself.*)

Future: for a time following the time of speaking or writing.
1. He *will leave* in a moment.
2. I *shall go* soon.

Few people insist upon the traditional grammatical distinction between *shall* (with *I* and *we*) and *will* (with *he, she, it, you, they*). For purposes of *emphasis,* or to suggest determination, you should say: I will, she shall, etc.

A rundown of the tenses, with examples:
Present: I leave, do leave, am leaving.

Past (simple): I left.

Future: I will leave.

Conditional: I would leave. (I would leave if I could.)

Present perfect (or perfect): I have left.

Past perfect: I had left.

Future perfect: I will have left. (By this time tomorrow, I will have left.)

Conditional perfect: I would have left. (If you had demanded it, I would have left by now.)

Progressive Forms: I am leaving; I was leaving; I will be leaving; I would be leaving; I have been leaving; I had been leaving; I will have been leaving; I would have been leaving. (The perfect forms of these progressives are rarely used, except perhaps for *I have been leaving:* Every day this month I have been leaving the house at eight.)

20.

THEME (MOTIF)—the subject on which one speaks or writes (hence college essays are known as themes). The term is used usually to indicate the *central* idea of a poem, story, play, novel, or essay. It is necessary, however, to distinguish between *theme, story,* and *plot.* The *theme* is the main idea; the *story* is the sequence of events or incidents—what happens. The *plot* is what happens or has happened or will happen to the characters, before or beyond the story.

20.

THERE, THEIR—Because these words are pronounced alike, they are often confused in writing. *There* is two things: an adverb indicating place, and an *expletive* (*which see*) that starts a sentence. *Their* is a possessive pronoun (called by some grammarians a possessive adjective). Do not confuse *they're*, or *they are*, with *there* and *their* because of similar pronunciation. Examples:

1. His coat is *there*, beyond the table. (*There* as adverb of place.)

2. *There* are two dogs in the kitchen eating garbage. (*There* is an expletive, to get the sentence started. The subject of this sentence is *two dogs*.)

3. *Their* outfits deserve attention. (*Their* as possessive pronoun or adjective.)

   Summation of similar words:

There's—There is

Theirs—possessive pronoun (I have *theirs*—meaning their books, etc.)

There're—There are

Their—possessive pronoun or adjective (I have *their* books.)

They're—They are

20.

THESIS—(1) in the classroom, a proposition or argument in an essay or a theme that one attempts to prove; (2) in a college or university, an undergraduate or graduate paper of some length that becomes the final stage of the degree; (3) in philosophy, the first stage of a dialectic or conflict of opposites, associated with Hegelian and Marxist thought. In graduate school, the thesis is usually at the master's level, whereas the dissertation is the long paper at the doctoral level.

20.

THIS & THESE, THAT & THOSE—in writing, these words refer to something already mentioned or to something immediately to be mentioned. Watch out for agreement (number):

> this (singular), these (plural)
> that (singular), those (plural)

1. There were several incidents on Pahlavi Avenue *that* day, but fortunately *these* incidents were not serious. (*These* keeps it immediate; *Those* would make it distant.)
2. *These* are the books you should read. (*These* at hand, here.)
3. *That* boy struck me. (*That* one, over there.)
4. *Those* girls are enjoying their stay in the country. (*Those* in the distance or in time.)

20.

TONE—from the Greek *tonos* ("stretching, tension"), tone in writing is determined by the author's attitude toward his listeners. He chooses or arranges his words differently as his audience varies, in recognition of his relation to it. The tone of his utterance reflects his awareness of this relation, his sense of how he stands toward those he is addressing. For instance, the tone of a gossip columnist may be confidential; of a teacher to a class, strict; of a funeral orator, solemn; of a satirist, ironical. In *Practical Criticism,* I. A. Richards, the philosopher and literary critic, places tone (along with sense, feeling, and intention) among the four kinds of meaning in any utterance.

20.

TRAGEDY—In his *Poetics,* Aristotle defined tragedy as "an imitation of an action that is complete, and whole, and of a certain magnitude." Tragedy is a sequence in which the chief figure (or protagonist) by some peculiarity of character (flaw or fault) passes through a series of misfortunes leading to a final catastrophe (his fall from power or position). The effect on the audience is *catharsis*—that is, through suffering fear and pity, the audience becomes aware of its own frailty and mortality. Classical tragedy occurred when a man or woman tried to approach the power and immortality of the gods.

20.

TRANSITION—a passage or movement from one state or stage to another. In writing, transition (a word or phrase or entire sentence) carries the writer from one subject to another smoothly and logically. Abrupt shifts from one subject to another create disconnected prose. Some common transitional words and phrases are: *however, consequently, in this manner, as a result, for example, hence, on the contrary, as we have noted or seen.* Also, transition can be achieved by repetition of a key word or phrase from a previous sentence. Transitions are especially necessary when the writer moves from one paragraph to the next. (On occasion, the writer needs an entire paragraph for transition from one idea to another, especially if the logical relationship of the ideas is not clear.)

22.

VERBLESS SENTENCE—term often used for any group of words that conveys a complete meaning even though there is no finite verb in the statement, as: What nerve! Tennis, anyone? Anything else? Such a slip of a thing! Although these are sentence fragments, they really serve as complete thoughts and are not incorrect. They should not be used too frequently in a given paper.

22.

VERBS—Verbs tell us something about the subject; they express states of feeling (such as *am, feel, sense*), or indicate action (such as *walk, run, strive*), or processes (*grow, develop, become*). If you are unsure of whether the word is a verb, put *he, she,* or *it* in front of it. If the result makes sense, you have a verb: She *walks* to the store. But: She *beautiful* every day of the week (makes no sense). *Warning:* Be sure to put a final *s* or *-es* in the present third person singular: *She* walk*s*, he swim*s*, she rush*es*. That final *s* indicates the *singular* form, not the plural.

There are several questions you can ask about a verb, as below:

CLASS: Is the verb transitive, intransitive, or linking?

Transitive: A transitive verb takes a direct object. He *threw the football.*

Intransitive: An intransitive verb takes no direct object. She *swims* in the river.

Linking (or *copulative*): A linking verb connects its subject with a noun that repeats it or an adjective that describes it. *She is* an *engineer.* (*Engineer* repeats *she.*) *He is* quite *tall.* (*Tall* describes *he.*)

NUMBER: Is the verb singular or plural? She *drives* to work every day. (Singular verb.) He and his brother *study* together. (Plural verb.) The subject of the verb will determine its number.

PERSON: Is the verb first, second, or third person? First person: I *am* pleased with your work. (*I* is first person.) Second person: You *may not come* any longer. (*You* is second person.) Third person: They *decided* against the proposal. (*They,* as well as *he, she, it,* is third person.)

TENSE: What is the verb's tense? Verbs have numerous tenses. (*See* TENSE.)

VOICE: Is the verb active or passive? We divide verbs into active and passive. In your writing, try to stress the active voice. *In the active, the subject commits the action. In the passive voice, the subject receives the action.* Use of an active-voice verb drives the sentence forward, whereas the passive-voice verb stalls it. See from the examples:

1. John *hit* the ball as hard as he could. (Active.)
2. The ball *was hit* by John as hard as he could. (Passive.)
3. She *did* the work as called for. (Active.)
4. The work *was done* (or *had been done*) by her as called for. (Passive.)

MOOD: What is the verb's mood? Every verb has a mood —the manner in which it is expressed. There are three possible moods: *indicative, subjunctive, imperative.*

Indicative: This is the mood we commonly use in writing and speaking. It indicates or states something. As: We *spoke* to the assembled group. Or: Harold *did* as he was told. Or: This *has been* a good party.

Subjunctive: This mood is very limited and appears mainly in contrary-to-fact statements. As: If I *were* wealthy, I would buy a yacht. (*Were* instead of *was.*) Or: I wish I *were* capable of doing that work. (*Were* instead of *was.*) In both instances, the speaker is saying something contrary to the fact: he is not wealthy and is not capable of doing that work.

Imperative: This mood appears chiefly in commands. As: *Be* good. *Take* care that you don't foul up.

There is one other area that you should be familiar with: the distinction between regular and irregular verbs. Regular verbs add *ed* to the past tense (*walk* becomes *walked*) and to the past participle (I have *walked*). Irregular verbs form their past tense in other ways (*sing* becomes *sang, is* becomes *was*); also, their past participles are irregular: I have *swum;* I have *been;* I have *gone.*

23.

WHOSE, WHO'S—*whose* is the possessive of *who; who's* is a contraction of *who is* or *who has*. The two should be carefully differentiated in writing:

1. Julius Caesar is the man *whose* will is unbendable. (*Whose* refers to *man.*)

2. Julius Caesar is the man *who's* assassinated in the Shakespeare play. (*Who's* is a contraction of *who is.*)

3. *Who's* got the answer to the riddle? (*Who's* is a contraction of *who has.*)

23.

WORDINESS—the practice of using more words than are necessary to express a thought. Brevity is not only the soul of wit, it is essential to mature writing. Below are sentences that would profit from rigorous pruning:

1. Basketball, as it is played today, is the number-one sport in the country. It is popular with both the players and the spectators. (Drop *as it is played today* and merge the two sentences into one: Basketball is the country's most popular sport with players and spectators alike.)

2. Basically, there are two things wrong with the modern automobile: in the first place, it is too expensive, and in the second, it is far too big. (Change to: Basically, two things are wrong with the automobile: it is too expensive and too big.)

23.

WOULD—indicates the future or a conditional situation.
1. My friend said that he *would* visit tomorrow. (The future is indicated; *would* is necessary after the past tense *said*.)
2. I *would* have baked you a cake if I had known you were coming. (A condition is established—of someone coming.)

Also, use *would* for habitual past action: He *would* often quote Shakespeare's epigrams.

Caution: Do not use *would* when the present or future tense of the verb is called for. I know that she *will* do well. (Use *will* after the present tense *know*.)

A Course of Grammar

The main elements of the traditional grammar course follow. The index will furnish any cross references not listed here in the main categories. For example, "voice" will be found in the index, which will lead the student to the entry VERBS.

I. *Parts of Speech:* Listed and outlined in 16. and alphabetically under each part of speech

II. *Main Sentence Elements:* Subject (19.)
Verb (22.)
Object: Direct, Indirect, Object of Preposition (15.)

III. *Phrases:* Prepositional, Infinitive, Participial, Gerund (16.)

IV. *Clauses:* Main and Subordinate (3.)

V. *Kinds of Sentence:* Simple, Compound, Complex, Compound-Complex (19.)

VI. *Fragments* (6.), *Comma Splice or Fault* (3.), *Run-on or Run-Together Sentence* (18.)

VII. *Verbals:* See Gerund (7.), Participle (16.), Infinitive (9.), and Dangling Modifier (4.)

VIII. *Agreement of Elements:* Subject and Verb (1.), Pronoun and Antecedent (1.)

IX. *Verbs* (22.) and *Tenses* (20.)

X. *Pronouns:* Personal, Possessive, Demonstrative, Relative, Reflexive (16.)

XI. *Punctuation:* See under alphabetical listings: comma, semicolon, colon, quotation marks, etc.

XII. *Outline* (3., at end of entry, and 18., at end of entry)

XIII. *Composition:* Organization of Ideas, Paragraphing, Topic Sentence, Development (3.)

XIV. *Research or Library Paper:* Choice of Topic, Outline, Use of Library, Bibliography, Footnoting (18.)

XV. *The Letter:* Application for a Job, Information About a School or Program of Instruction (12.)

Exercises

I. & II. *Parts of Speech & Main Sentence Elements*

See examples for *Tense* (20.):

    Pick out pronouns in 1,2,3 (at top)
               prepositions
               nouns
               adjectives
               adverbs
               conjunctions

See examples for *Parallelism* (16.)

    Pick out all verbs in 1–6
               subjects
               objects of preposition
               indirect objects
               direct objects
               prepositions
               conjunctions

See examples for *Sentence Variety* (19.)

    Pick out subjects in (1) A–D
               prepositional phrases
    Pick out verbs in (2) A–C
    Pick out direct objects in (3) A–D
    Pick out conjunctions in all of the above

III. & IV. *Phrases and Clauses*

See examples for Style (19.)

    Pick out prepositional phrases in 1–10
               subordinate clauses
               participial phrases
               prepositional phrases

See examples for Parallelism (16.)

    Pick out main clauses in 1–6
               gerund phrases

> infinitive phrases
> subordinate clauses
> participial phrases

V. *Kinds of Sentence* (Simple, Compound, Complex, Compound-Complex)

List kinds of sentence in the definitions of Rhythm (18.), Plagiarism (16.), and Metaphor (13.)

VI. *Fragments, Comma Splice or Fault, Run-on or Run-Together Sentences*

See *Composition* (3.), sentences A–J:

> Turn each of these fragments into a correct sentence. Avoid comma faults and run-ons in so doing.

VII. *Verbals*

See examples for *Parallelism* (16.)

> Pick out participles in 1–6
> > gerunds
> > infinitives
> > any dangling modifiers

See examples for *Style* (19.)

> Pick out all verbals used only as verbals (not as part of the verb) in 1–10

VIII. *Agreement of Elements*

In the definition of *Awkward* (1.), identify all agreement of subject and verb and pronouns and their antecedents.

IX. *Verbs and Tenses*

Identify all verbs and their tenses in the definitions of *Expository Writing* (5.), *Fiction* (6.), and *Image* and *Imagery* (9.).

X. *Pronouns*

Identify all pronouns in *Research Paper* (18.)

XI. *Punctuation*

Justify every mark of punctuation in the definition of *Character* (3.) Show how some sentences can be joined by semicolons.

Justify each comma in the definition of *Wordiness* (23.), *Fiction* (6), and *Narrative* (14.).

Write five sentences using semicolons, on the model of the definition of the *semicolon* (19.).

INDEX

188

189

190

ABOUT THE AUTHORS

A graduate of Cornell and Columbia Universities, Leo Hamalian is a professor of English at the City College of New York. He has also taught at the California Institute of the Arts, the University of Damascus, and the University of Tehran. He has conducted writing workshops and his articles and poems have appeared in national publications. He has co-edited eleven modern short novels, *The Existential Imagination, The Naked i, The Radical Vision, Solo,* and *New Writing from the Middle East,* and has co-authored *Grammar in Context.* A collection of his essays appeared in 1978 entitled *Burn After Reading.* He edits the literary quarterly *Ararat,* and lives in Manhattan.

A Professor of English, Frederick R. Karl has been at the City College of New York for twenty years. He has taught the full range of courses, from graduate seminars to courses in Basic Writing and English as a Second Language (for foreign-born students). Recipient of a Guggenheim Fellowship and a Fulbright lectureship in American literature (to France), he is the author of several books on the novel: *A Reader's Guide to Joseph Conrad, The Contemporary English Novel,* and *The Adversary Literature.* He has, also, co-edited (with Professor Hamalian) several anthologies, including *The Fourth World, The Shape of Fiction, Short Fiction of the Masters, The Naked i,* and *The Radical Vision.* He is currently engaged in editing the Collected Letters of Joseph Conrad.